# TRACING YOUR NONCONFORMIST ANCESTORS

# FAMILY HISTORY FROM PEN & SWORD

# TRACING YOUR NONCONFORMIST ANCESTORS

*A Guide for Family and Local Historians*

Stuart A. Raymond

Pen & Sword
**FAMILY HISTORY**

First published in Great Britain in 2017
PEN & SWORD FAMILY HISTORY
an imprint of
Pen & Sword Books Ltd
47 Church Street,
Barnsley South Yorkshire, S70 2AS

ISBN 978 1 47388 345 1

A CIP catalogue record for this book is
available from the British Library.

Typeset in Palatino and Optima by CHIC GRAPHICS

Printed and bound in England by
CPI Group (UK), Croydon, CR0 4YY

Pen & Sword Books Ltd incorporates the imprints of Pen & Sword
Archaeology, Atlas, Aviation, Battleground, Discovery, Family History,
History, Maritime, Military, Naval, Politics, Railways, Select, Social History,
Transport, True Crime, Claymore Press, Frontline Books, Leo Cooper,
Praetorian Press, Remember When, Seaforth Publishing and Wharncliffe.

For a complete list of Pen & Sword titles please contact
PEN & SWORD BOOKS LTD
47 Church Street, Barnsley, South Yorkshire, S70 2AS, England
E-mail: enquiries@pen-and-sword.co.uk
Website: www.pen-and-sword.co.uk

# CONTENTS

# ABBREVIATIONS

| | |
|---|---|
| BMS | Baptist Missionary Society |
| *IGI* | *International Genealogical Index* |
| LDS | Latter Day Saints (Mormons) |
| MARC | Methodist Archives and Research Centre |
| SOAS | School of Oriental and African Studies |
| SoG | Society of Genealogists |

# INTRODUCTION AND ACKNOWLEDGEMENTS

The aim of this book is to introduce family and local historians to the archives of the historic Nonconformist denominations of England and Wales. It covers all of the major denominations and also includes mention of many minor denominations, such as the Christadelphians and the Muggletonians. It does not, however, deal with the numerous new denominations established in the late twentieth century, although some sources relevant to that period are mentioned.

Many website addresses (URLs) are mentioned in the following pages. However, URLs change frequently. In order to identify any websites whose URLs have changed, simply search the title of the website at **www.google.com**. Alternatively, you may be able to find a copy of the original webpage by searching the old URL at the Wayback Machine **https://archive.org**.

This book has been in preparation for almost a decade. My thanks to Roger Thorne, who greatly encouraged me when I first began writing, gave me access to his library and read an early draft. One of my former students also read an early draft and made many useful suggestions.

# Chapter 1

# THE HISTORY OF NONCONFORMITY

Jesus prayed for his followers 'that they may all be one'.[1] Sadly, His prayer has frequently been ignored. The church has been divided since the clash between Peter and Paul mentioned in the Acts of the Apostles. Ever since that clash, both the doctrine and the practice of Christianity have been much disputed, and the fact that the Christian God is a God of love has frequently been lost sight of in bitter disputes that should have been judged in the light of that love.

In England, tradition assigns the foundation of the church to Aristobulus in the first century, although adequate evidence is lacking. Disputes wracked the Celtic church. In the late fourth century, Pelagius, who was born in Britain, denied the doctrine of original sin, caused major controversy and was denounced as a heretic. Several centuries later, when missionaries from Rome arrived in Canterbury, they found that the practices of Roman and Celtic traditions differed considerably and much bitterness was caused by a dispute over the date of Easter. By the end of the seventh century, however, the two traditions had fused and England enjoyed a remarkably long period without any serious division within the church.

That period ended at the end of the fourteenth century, with the rise of the Lollard 'heresy'. The Lollards took their inspiration from John Wycliffe. He emphasized the individual's right to interpret the Bible for himself, challenged the privileged status of the clergy and denounced the wealth and pomp surrounding the church and its services. He was also the first person since King Alfred to attempt a translation of the Bible into English.

The Lollards, with the Continental Anabaptists of the early sixteenth century, were the spiritual forebears of those who sought separation from the established church on theological grounds. They were the original exponents of non-liturgical worship – silence, prophesyings and open prayer – as was subsequently practised by the Quakers. It may be that some later separatist churches were directly descended from Lollard groups. Such churches were persecuted and therefore did not keep records, but the fact that the first General Baptist church was located in Coventry, which had been a strong Lollard area, is suggestive. However, there is much academic dispute as to whether particular Lollard congregations survived until the Reformation.[2] Local historians are well placed to search for evidence which may demonstrate continuity.

Many Wycliffite ideas were reformulated by men such as Martin Luther and John Calvin in the early sixteenth century. Initially, these Protestants found little support in England. However, Henry VIII's desperate search for allies in his divorce proceedings led him to appoint Thomas Cromwell as his chief minister and Thomas Cranmer as his Archbishop of Canterbury. Both were Protestants. Their appointments lit the fuses that led to the English Reformation. The Church of England separated from the Roman Catholic Church and gradually adopted Protestant tenets. The process was not without its hiccups and Queen Mary tried to reverse it altogether. Her failure to do so was due to her early death and lack of a Roman Catholic heir. The accession of the Protestant Elizabeth led to a new ecclesiastical settlement which achieved finality due to the longevity of her reign. It was a compromise between a fairly conservative Queen and Calvinistic bishops who had just returned from exile in Geneva. The Queen established her own religious policy, but had to rely on bishops who did not necessarily agree with her to implement it.

On one point, however, the Queen and her bishops agreed, and so did their successors for the next century or so. They placed great emphasis on the importance of uniformity. Sectarianism was not to be tolerated. Tolerance for different beliefs – whether Protestant or Catholic – was regarded as dangerous for both the security of the state and the health of the church. Indeed, Roman Catholicism did pose a serious threat, as was demonstrated by the Spanish Armada and the Gunpowder Plot. Everyone was required to worship together in their parish church, Sunday by Sunday. And the worship that was required was to be in accordance with Cranmer's *Book of Common Prayer*.

Many Calvinists (who came to be known as Puritans) regarded the Elizabethan church as but half reformed and wished to adopt a more Presbyterian form of church government, that is, government by representative assemblies of elders, rather than by bishops. They attached great importance to sermons, and objected to many ceremonies which Charles I's Archbishop of Canterbury, William Laud, and other bishops sought to enforce, arguing that they pointed towards Rome. But their aim was to convert the Church of England, not to separate from it. Calvinistic Puritans under Elizabeth and the early Stuarts were the spiritual forebears of those Nonconformists who sought reformation within the established church, rather than separation. There were few Elizabethan separatists. The church hierarchy, however, gradually turned against Puritanism, especially under Laud. His attempts to emphasize the 'beauty of holiness' in outward ceremonial met considerable resistance; Puritans regarded it as Papist.

The Civil War was not, in origin, a religious war. According to Richard Baxter, one of the leading Nonconformist divines, 'religion was not the thing first contested for'. Puritans, however, were amongst the leading Parliamentarians, and they took the opportunity to dismantle the entire structure of episcopal governance. There was an attempt to replace it with a Presbyterian structure, based on the Westminster Confession of 1646, but that proved impossible to achieve. The Independents were too powerful; their Savoy Declaration of 1658 modified the Presbyterian statement and set out their own attitude to the national church. However, the failure to impose a uniform system of ecclesiastical governance during the Interregnum permitted a vast array of radical ideas and beliefs to receive public airing. Numerous sects were formed, for example the Ranters, the Fifth Monarchists, the Muggletonians, the Baptists and

*From* A Catalogue of the Severall Sects and Opinions in England and other Nations With a briefe Rehearsall of their false and dangerous Tenents *(1647)*.

the Quakers. Mostly, such groups operated outside of parochial structures. Religion was increasingly seen as a matter between the individual and his maker, not as a matter between the subject and the Crown (or the Protector).

Most of these sects were small in numbers and lacked significant gentry support. The Ranters believed that they were incapable of sinning and that therefore they could do what they liked. They do not seem to have had any organization (if indeed they ever existed[3]) and were repressed by the Interregnum regime. The Fifth Monarchists survived the Restoration, but were wiped out as a result of Venner's Rising in 1661. Some other minor sects lingered on, despite the repression imposed by the Cavalier Parliament. The Muggletonians were still in existence in the twentieth century, but their impact was so small that no historian was aware of them until their (extensive) archives were discovered and placed in the British Library in the 1970s.

Other sects were stronger. The Quakers were beginning to develop an organizational structure by 1660.[4] They suffered greater persecution under Charles II than other Dissenters, due to their refusal to swear the oath of allegiance, to pay tithes or to acknowledge their 'superiors' by taking off their hats. Nevertheless,

Quakers survived their many 'sufferings', as they called them. A number of Baptist and Independent congregations also managed to survive Cavalier persecution. For example, the Baptists of Southwick (Wiltshire) formed their church in 1655. During the years of persecution, they met in a secluded wood owned by a sympathetic landowner.[5]

These sects mostly ignored the parochial structure and established their own churches. They were not prepared to be absorbed into either a Presbyterian system of church government or into Charles II's restored Church of England. Presbyterians, however, had operated within the parochial system and many held incumbencies. They had mostly welcomed the Restoration and bitterly attacked Quakers and other radical sects. They (mistakenly) relied on Charles II's Declaration of Breda of 1660, which had promised them religious liberty, and thought themselves to be in a strong position to influence

*George Fox refusing to take his oath in 1663. From a painting by John Pettie.*

the restored Church of England and to negotiate the establishment of a modified episcopacy. Charles's promise, however, was not kept. He was sympathetic, but lacked the political strength to protect them against vengeful Cavaliers and high Anglicans. The Cavalier Parliament refused to accept Puritan loyalties, or to introduce a modified form of episcopacy. When the Act of Uniformity, 1662, made the use of the *Book of Common Prayer* compulsory in all church services, required all clergy to accept episcopal ordination, and obliged them to deny the validity of the Solemn League and Covenant – which many of them had sworn to during the Civil War – some 2,000 ministers refused to comply and were ejected from their parochial livings. Their ejection transformed the Nonconformist cause, giving it the strength it needed to survive and flourish. Without them, Nonconformity would have consisted of a handful of separatists and the Quakers, with little influence. If the Cavalier Parliament had thought that Dissent would disappear with the ejection of Puritan clergy, they were to find themselves very mistaken.

Unlike most sectaries, the ejected clergy were men of some position. They were mostly university graduates and had some support amongst the gentry. Collectively, at least, they were men of influence possessing substantial resources. The Bishop of Exeter complained in 1663 that, in Devon, there were 'at least 14 Justices of the Peace who are accounted arrant Presbyterians'.[6] The ejected clergy found considerable support amongst their former parishioners and, despite the Clarendon Code (see below), were able to 'gather the saints'; some of their congregations survive to the present day. The early history of such churches is, of course, shrouded in mystery; their meetings had to be kept secret and they frequently kept no records. Surviving records are therefore those which derive from state surveillance.

After 1662, Presbyterians, Independents (subsequently known as Congregationalists) and Baptists sometimes worked closely with each other. The boundaries between these three denominations were fluid in the early years of Nonconformity; particular congregations frequently switched allegiance between them in the late seventeenth and eighteenth centuries. In 1672, Bunyan's church at Bedford,

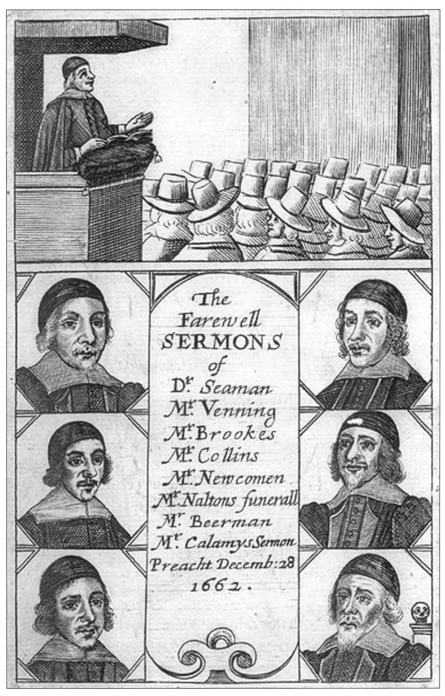

The
Farewell
SERMONS
of
Dr. Seaman
Mr. Venning
Mr. Brookes
Mr. Collins
Mr. Newcomen
Mr. Naltons funerall
Mr. Beerman
Mr. Calamys Sermon
Preacht Decemb: 28
1662.

*Farewell sermons from ministers ejected in 1662.*

7

which has historically been regarded as a Baptist church, described itself as being Congregational. As late as 1766, it was 'independent'.[7] It should also be borne in mind that most ejected ministers were not separatists: they had been forced out of the established church and hoped for a reunited Church of England in which they could play their part. It was not until the first generation had died out that the value of denominationalism became fully accepted amongst Nonconformist ministers.

Most Presbyterian congregations became Unitarian in the eighteenth century, as did some Congregationalists and Baptists. Indeed, some individual former Anglicans could also be found amongst the Unitarian ranks. Conversely, many orthodox Presbyterians transferred their allegiances to Congregational, Anglican and other churches. The histories of specific denominations are outlined in the chapters that follow.

The fluidity found amongst the 'three denominations' was not experienced by the Society of Friends (who are popularly known as Quakers). They had a much tighter organization, designed to withstand persecution and suffering. As a consequence, the Quaker paper trail is much more extensive than that of other denominations, and their history can be studied in much greater depth.

The religious legislation which followed the Restoration was known as the Clarendon Code, after the King's first minister, although it was more repressive than either the Earl of Clarendon, or the King, thought necessary. The Corporation Act of 1661 required all municipal officials to take Anglican communion and to formally reject the Solemn League and Covenant of 1643. This effectively excluded Nonconformists from public office. The Act of Uniformity of 1662 imposed a narrow ritualistic rigidity on the church (see above). The Conventicle Act of 1664 forbade meetings of five or more people for unauthorized worship, and the Five Mile Act of 1665 forbade Dissenting ministers from visiting incorporated towns or the places where they had previously held incumbencies. These acts together enabled Justices of the Peace to fine and imprison Nonconformists who sought to practise their faith. As we will, see, they produced much documentation.

The penal aspects of these laws were suspended by Charles II's Declaration of Indulgence in 1672, which permitted Nonconformists to hold their meetings subject to obtaining a licence (for licences, see below, p.43–4). Some 1,600 licences were issued, including c. 1,000 to Presbyterian ministers. The suspension did not last long: Parliament forced the King to withdraw both the Declaration and the licences issued under it. Persecution resumed, especially after the 1685 Monmouth Rebellion in the South-West.[8] However, the penal acts were again suspended by James II in 1687, this time permanently. His motive in doing so was to remove the threat of prosecution from Roman Catholics; consequently many Nonconformists, bitterly opposed to Roman Catholicism, felt uncomfortable in accepting James's Declaration. The difficulty was not, however, to last for very long. Anglicans too felt threatened by James II's Roman Catholicism; when William of Orange invaded in 1688, most Anglicans were on the same side as the Dissenters. The latter were rewarded with the Toleration Act of 1689, which permanently suspended the penal statutes. This marked a major turning point in Nonconformist history. They could now worship openly, erect chapels, baptise infants and administer communion. They registered thousands of meeting houses. By 1715, there were at least 400,000 Dissenters.[9]

The Test Acts, denying Nonconformists public office, remained in place until 1828. Many Nonconformists got around this by practising occasional conformity, attending an Anglican communion service merely in order to obtain a sacrament certificate confirming they had done so, and thus entitling them to enter public office.[10] They could do so with a clear conscience; Nonconformists like Baxter had no theological objections to participating in Anglican services.

Occasional conformity was not ideal, however and could not be practised by groups such as the Quakers. Other grievances also remained after 1689. Everyone was required to pay tithes to their Church of England incumbents and church rates to their churchwardens, regardless of their denominational allegiance. Unitarians were particularly aggrieved at being compelled to use a marriage liturgy designed for believers in the Trinity. The politics of education in the nineteenth century was bedeviled by the competition for control between Anglicans and Nonconformists. From 1662, the universities of both Oxford and Cambridge required students to subscribe to the doctrine and government of the Church of England before they could graduate. Oxford also required them to subscribe to the Thirty-Nine Articles and to swear the Oath of Supremacy before they matriculated. Another grievance was to be created in 1753, when Hardwicke's Marriage Act required all marriages other than those of Quakers and Jews to be conducted by an Anglican priest.

These grievances were gradually removed in the nineteenth century. The Civil Registration Act of 1836 enabled Nonconformists to marry in the presence of a registrar. It also enabled births to be recorded in civil registers, rather than in the baptismal registers of the Church of England, although it was not until 1898 that Nonconformists (other than the Quakers) were able to marry in their own churches without the presence of a district registrar. The doctrinal tests for most students at Oxford were abolished in 1854, and at Cambridge in 1856. Elected school boards were created in 1870, and the competition between the denominations for control of education switched to the ballot box at school board elections. By the end of the century, Nonconformists were legally regarded as having equality with Anglicans, although admittedly the Church of England continued to be the established church – and remains so to this day.

The 'old Dissent' is a term which contrasts seventeenth-century denominations with those that arose as a result of the evangelical revival in the eighteenth and nineteenth centuries. Evangelicalism sought personal conversion from a life of sin to faith in God, leading to a life of activism in evangelism and social care, based on love for the Bible and trust in the atoning death of Christ on the cross. It was frequently denounced as 'enthusiasm', although John Wesley, its leading exponent, would have denied the charge. The sectarians of the mid-seventeenth century, of course, had been 'enthusiasts'; hence the distrust felt by the Anglican establishment.

At the same time that rationalism was leading many Presbyterians to Unitarianism, Wesley spent his life riding across the country

*John Wesley preaching outside a church.* (Courtesy Wellcome Images)

preaching the Gospel and creating the Wesleyan Methodist Connexion – although attempting to avoid a breach with the Church of England. His successors gave up the attempt and the denomination ceased to consider itself a society within the established church. After Wesley's death, the Wesleyan Methodists suffered a number of splits and a variety of Methodist denominations appeared. They all adopted the Wesleyan model of connexional governance. The breach with the Church of England continued to widen, but, as late as 1821, the Vicar of Bridgerule (Devon) told the Bishop of Exeter that in his parish Bible Christians were more regular in their attendance at church than his other parishioners. Methodists did not consider themselves to be Nonconformists and their successors still prefer the term 'free church'.

The effects of the evangelical revival were not confined to Methodism and the Church of England. Other Nonconformists were reinvigorated too. Their numbers had not increased after the removal of the penal laws. But when Congregationalists and Baptists began to imitate the Wesleyan use of itinerant preachers in the late eighteenth and early nineteenth centuries, their numbers grew.

The religious census of 1851 (see below, pp.39–41) demonstrates that Nonconformist numbers (both Methodist and old Dissenters), increased dramatically between 1781 and the mid-nineteenth century. The various Methodist denominations together had more than three times the number of chapels as their strongest rivals, the Congregationalists, although the numbers attending each chapel was lower. In Wales, no less than 87 per cent worshipped in Nonconformist churches. The Calvinistic Methodists were the strongest Welsh Nonconformist denomination. The various Baptist denominations were also relatively strong, but other denominations of the old dissent were weak. The old Presbyterian churches had mostly become Unitarian, although missionary endeavours from the Scottish Presbyterians had created a new Presbyterian denomination. By 1898, there were reported to be only about 200 villages without a Nonconformist chapel.[11]

## The Strength of the Major Nonconformist Denominations in 1851

| Denominations | Places of Worship | Worshippers as Percentage of Population |
|---|---|---|
| Methodists | 11,007 | 7.7% |
| Congregationalists | 3,244 | 4.4% |
| Baptists | 2,789 | 3.3% |
| Unitarians | 229 | 0.2% |
| Presbyterians (Scottish) | 160 | 0.2% |
| Quakers | 371 | 0.1% |

In the century after the census, a variety of new denominations came into being. The Salvation Army was founded by 'General' Booth in the late nineteenth century. A variety of other denominations also came into being as a result of evangelical revivals – the Plymouth Brethren, the Sandemanians, the Irvingites, the Catholic Apostolic Church and the Free Church of England, amongst others. The early twentieth century saw the beginnings of Pentecostalism. Some of these denominations are discussed in Chapters 6 and 8 below.

Evangelicalism promoted missionary activity overseas. A variety of overseas missionary societies were founded in the late eighteenth and nineteenth centuries. These are discussed in the appropriate denominational chapters below. The missionary impulse was not one way; two sects sent North American missionaries to England. Jehovah's Witnesses and the Latter Day Saints (who are still frequently referred to as Mormons), both preached versions of Christianity which were not recognized as Christian at all by most other denominations. These denominations are discussed in Chapter 8.

A variety of other foreign denominations also operated in England and Wales; these are considered in Chapter 7. Some of these were not technically 'Nonconformist' (although it is convenient to consider their records here), as they were accepted as legitimate by the Church of England. The Huguenots were the most significant group. The Moravians were also important, greatly influencing the Wesleyan revival. The validity of Moravian orders was recognized by Anglican bishops in 1749.

The Roman Catholic Church was also active in England and Wales. They would not have regarded themselves as Nonconformist; rather, they would have argued that it was the Church of England which failed to conform. Its clergy experienced ejection from their livings a century before the Nonconformist ejection of 1662. They had suffered under both Edward VI and Elizabeth, and continued to suffer persecution even as late as the nineteenth century; in Northern Ireland, prejudice against them continues to this day. Their experience, however, was wholly different to that of Protestant

Nonconformity, although the penal laws used against them were sometimes also used against Nonconformists. Roman Catholics will be considered in my forthcoming *Tracing your Roman Catholic Ancestors*.

Most of the denominations discussed here were open to ecumenism. Movement between them was frequent; if a Nonconformist moved to a place where there was no chapel of his denomination, he was likely to join a chapel of another denomination. In the eighteenth century, many Presbyterians joined other denominations rather than accepting their own congregation's move towards Unitarianism. Quakers who were disowned (see below, pp.128–9) were likely to join another denomination. Increasingly, towards the end of the nineteenth century, local Nonconformists joined together in free church councils. Only a few denominations refused to have anything to do with Christians of other denominations and considered that they alone were proclaiming the truth. Strict Baptists, the Exclusive Brethren and the Christadelphians all tended towards this position. Jehovah's Witnesses and the Mormons are modern examples of sects which would not even be regarded as Christian by most denominations.

In the last two decades of the nineteenth century, the numbers of Nonconformists as a proportion of the total population began to fall. That fall continued in the twentieth century. Increasing state provision of education and welfare, together with a widening of the range of social activities available outside of the churches, meant that the attraction of religious allegiance for the working classes was diminishing. Meanwhile, the congregations of many inner-city churches became gentrified, moved out to the suburbs and left a much diminished Nonconformist presence in city centres. Chapel for many ceased to be an all-encompassing way of life.

Nevertheless, Nonconformity survived and continues to play an important role in society. The impact of the eighteenth-century evangelical revival still reverberates in British society. It played a vital role in forming the Victorian social conscience and in the origins and history of twentieth century left-wing politics. Jeremy Corbyn owes a great deal to the Nonconformist tradition. The task of the local historian is to examine how these trends played out in the history of the local church and community. Family historians will want to discover how they played out in the lives of family members.

## A NOTE ON NOMENCLATURE
The nomenclature used to describe opponents of the established religion has varied over the centuries. Originally, Nonconformists were those who adhered to the doctrine, but not the usages, of the Church of England. In 1662, the term was applied to those clergy who refused to conform to the Restoration settlement and who were consequently ejected from their livings. It was subsequently extended to include all English and Welsh Protestants who were members of denominations other than the Church of England. Incidentally, one of the major differences between Anglicans and Nonconformists is that everyone in England was legally regarded as a member of the Church of England: they had no choice in the matter. Nonconformists, however, chose the denomination they wished to join. Many of them also changed their denomination when they married or moved house – especially when there was no chapel of their original denomination in the immediate vicinity. Chapel was chapel, whatever its formal label.[12]

The term 'Dissenter' was frequently used synonymously with 'Nonconformist', although the former was sometimes restricted to those groups who dissented from the principle of an established church. The Independents, the Baptists and the Quakers had all insisted on separation and were proud to accept the label 'Dissenter'. Such groups are also sometimes described as 'separatists'.

The term 'sectarian' is another term that was loosely used as synonymous with Dissenter. It is better to reserve this term for groups such as the Exclusive Brethren and the Strict Baptists, who wish to have nothing to do with other Christian denominations. The Jehovah's Witnesses take sectarianism to its logical conclusion – although the majority of mainstream Christians would deny that they were Christian.

Presbyterians preferred to be known as Nonconformists; they wanted to be part of the established church, but not on the terms which were on offer. Baxter described himself as a 'half-Dissenter'. Some groups, especially Methodists, vigorously denied that they were either Dissenters or Nonconformists, although they were happy to use the term 'free church'.

'Puritan' was another frequently used term, originally applied sarcastically to devout Protestants. Puritans were known for the importance which they attached to personal religion, for strictness and gravity of behaviour and for plainness of dress and manners. Most sixteenth-century Puritans, as we have already seen, were Calvinists, not separatists. They were, however, the precursors of Nonconformity as it developed after the Restoration.

## FURTHER READING

Nonconformity has a huge literature, but the researcher needs to be aware that many older works are apologetical in character, written to defend the specific denomination or cause the author supports, rather than being objective studies. There are, however, many works which do meet modern standards of criticism. Nonconformity is placed in its context by:

- Edwards, David L. *Christian England*. (Rev ed. Fount Paperbacks, 1989).
- Rosman, Doreen. *The Evolution of the English Churches*. (Cambridge University Press, 2003).
- Southern, Antonia. *House divided: Christianity in England, 1526-1829*. (Academic Press, 2014).

The authoritative modern introduction to dissent is:

- Watts, Michael R. *The Dissenters*. (3 vols. Clarendon Press, 1978–2015).

A briefer overview is provided by:

- Sangster, Paul. *A History of the Free Churches*. (Heinemann, 1983).

Some useful essays are included in:

- Nuttall, Geoffrey F. *Studies in English Dissent.* (Quinta Press, 2002).
- Nuttall, Geoffrey F., & Chadwick, Owen, eds. *From Uniformity to Unity, 1662-1962.* (SPCK, 1962).
- Pope, Robert, ed. *T & T. Clark Companion to Nonconformity.* (Blooomsbury, 2013).
- Spufford, Margaret, ed. *The World of Rural Dissenters, 1520-1725.* (Cambridge University Press, 1995).

For a discussion of the Great Ejection, its antecedents and its aftermath, see:

- Sell, Alan P.F., ed. *The Great Ejection of 1662: its antecedents, aftermath and ecumenical significance.* (Pickwick Publications, 2012).

Post-Restoration Nonconformity is discussed in:

- Brown, Raymond. *Spirituality in Adversity: English Nonconformity in a Period of Repression, 1660-1689.* (Paternoster Press, 2012).
- Nuttall, Geoffrey, et al, eds. *The Beginnings of Nonconformity.* (James Clarke & Co., 1964).

For the eighteenth century, see:

- Bradley, J.E. *Religion, Revolution and English Radicalism: Nonconformity in Eighteenth-Century politics and Society.* (Cambridge University Press, 1990).
- Noll, Mark. *The Rise of Evangelicalism: the age of Edwards, Whitefield and the Wesleys.* (Apollos, 2004).

A general history of evangelicalism is provided by:

- Bebbington, D.W. *Evangelicalism in Modern Britain: a history from the 1730s to the 1980s.* (Unwin Hyman, 1989).

The growth of itinerant ministries during the evangelical revival is discussed in:

- Lovegrove, Deryck W. *Established Church, Sectarian People: Itinerancy and the Transformation of English Dissent, 1780-1830.* (Cambridge University Press, 1988).

For nineteenth-century Nonconformity, good brief introductions are provided by:

- Bebbington, David. *Victorian Nonconformity.* (Lutterworth Press, 2011).
- Sellers, Ian. *Nineteenth-century Nonconformity.* (Edward Arnold, 1977).

An overview of religion in Victorian Britain, with many useful articles, can be found at:

- The Victorian Web: Literature, History and Culture in the Age of Victoria
  **www.victorianweb.org/religion**

Some more substantial works are provided by:

- Binfield, Clyde. *So Down to Prayers: Studies in English Nonconformity, 1780-1920.* (J.M. Dent & Sons, 1977).
- Johnson, Dale A. *The Changing Shape of English Nonconformity, 1825-1925.* (Oxford University Press, 1999).

For nineteenth-century evangelicalism, see:

- Bebbington, David W. *The Dominance of Evangelicalism: the Age of Spurgeon and Moody.* (Inter Varsity Press, 2005).
- Wolffe, John. *The Expansion of Evangelicalism: the Age of Wilberforce, More, Chalmers and Finney.* (Inter-Varsity Press, 2006).

For the twentieth century, see:

- Sell, Alan P.F., & Cross, Anthony R., eds. *Protestant Nonconformity in the Twentieth Century*. (Paternoster Press, 2003).

The history of overseas mission is discussed by:

- Cox, Jeffrey. *The British Missionary Enterprise since 1700*. (Routledge, 2008).
- Stanley, Brian. *The Bible and the Flag: Protestant Missions and British Imperialism in the Nineteenth and Twentieth Centuries*. (Apollos, 1990).

For Christian mission in its wider context, see Part 2 of:

- Neill, Stephen. *A History of Christian Mission*. Penguin History of the Church, 6. (2nd ed. Penguin, 1986).

There are a number of local studies which should be read by all researchers as models of what can be done. These include, for example:

- Brockett, Allan. *Nonconformity in Exeter, 1650-1875*. (Manchester University Press, 1962).
- Obelkevich, James. *Religion and Rural Society, 1825-1975*. (Clarendon Press, 1976).
- Urdank, Albion M. *Religion and Society in a Cotswold Vale: Nailsworth, Gloucestershire, 1780-1865*. (University of California Press, 1998). Downloadable from **http://publishing.cdlib.org/ucpressebooks**

There are numerous bibliographies of Nonconformity, many of them covering specific denominations. The latter are listed in the appropriate chapter below. For an extensive general bibliography, consult:

• Field, Clive D. 'Sources for Protestant Nonconformity in England and Wales since 1662: a structured bibliography', in Pope, Robert, ed. *T. & T. Clark Companion to Nonconformity*. (Bloomsbury, 2013), pp.495–532.

Many valuable local studies are available in unpublished theses. Recent theses can be identified by consulting:

• History On-Line: Theses
  **www.history.ac.uk/history-online/theses**

Many theses are available online at:

• EThOS: E theses Online service
  **http://ethos.bl.uk/Home.do**

Nonconformist historians have produced an enormous body of literature on the local history of Dissent. A variety of bibliographies and guides to this literature are noted where appropriate in the following chapters. The general histories noted above and in the denominational chapters provide the background information needed by local and family historians. There are also a number of regional histories which include historical accounts of particular congregations. See, for example:

• Evans, George Eyre. *Midland Churches: a history of the congregations on the roll of the Midland Christian Union*. (Herald, 1899).
• Nightingale, Benjamin. *Lancashire Nonconformity, or sketches historical and descriptive of the Congregational and old Presbyterian churches in the county*. (6 vols. 1890–3).

The transactions of county historical societies, such as the Devonshire Association, also have many relevant articles. However, the vast proportion of Nonconformist historical literature is concerned with the history of particular congregations. Most churches have produced their own histories, or at least commemorative brochures. Thorne has described these as 'rarely impartial, seldom critical, often slight, often indifferently printed or duplicated, often written in a homely style and often difficult to locate'. They do, however, benefit from the fact that their authors have normally had access to the collective memories of fellow worshippers, which may extend back for half a century or more. They are also likely to have had access to records in church safes, which may be hidden away from other researchers. These local church histories should be sought out in local studies libraries and record offices, and in the libraries of institutions specialising in Nonconformist church history. Some have been digitized for the internet.

Some information may also be available in general local histories for particular places. That is not, however, invariably the case. The otherwise authoritative *Victoria County History* paid limited attention to Nonconformist history prior to 1949, although it currently aims to mention every Nonconformist community. See:

- Pugh, R.B. 'The Victoria History of the counties of England', *Baptist Quarterly* 27(3), 1977, pp.110–17.
- Victoria History of the Counties of England
  **www.victoriacountyhistory.ac.uk/counties**

Numerous *Victoria County History* volumes are available online at:

- British History Online
  **history.ac.uk/projects/digital/british-history-online**

Many local histories were written by Anglican clergy and other churchmen, who sometimes ignored the Nonconformists amongst them. For example, Kilkhampton (Cornwall) was in the heartland of the Bible Christian movement, but there is no mention of Methodism whatsoever in Dew's *A History of the Parish and Church of Kilkhampton* (2nd ed. 1926). Dew was the rector of the parish. A subsequent author wrote a whole book on Kilkhampton Methodism.[13]

In order to track down such local histories as exist, researchers should first consult any relevant bibliographies (see the comment above). There are historical bibliographies for most counties, which are likely to identify substantial histories of particular churches. They are listed in:

• Lester, Ray, et al, eds. *The New Walford Guide to Reference Resources, Vol. 2: The Social Sciences*. (Facet Publishing, 2007).

The county volumes of the present author's series of *British Genealogical Library Guides* (formerly *British Genealogical Bibliographies*) aim to list all local publications likely to be of use to family historians. Counties covered include Buckinghamshire, Cheshire, Cornwall, Cumberland, Dorset, Devon, Essex, Gloucestershire, Hampshire, Kent, Lancashire, London, Middlesex, Norfolk, Oxfordshire, Somerset, Suffolk, Surrey, Sussex, Westmorland, Wiltshire and Yorkshire.

Dr. Williams's Library holds many local church histories; these will be listed in its online catalogue when it is complete (see below, p.32); until then, see:

• *Nonconformist congregations in Great Britain: a list of histories and other material in Dr. Williams's Library*. (Dr. Williams's Trust, 1973).

A model county bibliography devoted specifically to Nonconformist local history (and listing much ephemeral material) is provided by:

• Thorne, Roger F.S. 'Our providential way: a bibliography of the history of Dissent in Devon', *Devonshire Association ... transactions* 127, 1995, pp.201–46.

*Chapter 2*

# SOURCES FOR NONCONFORMITY

The records of English and Welsh churches other than the Church of England are extensive, and offer family and local historians many opportunities for research. In 1851, there were no less than 113 distinct denominations in England and Wales, with 22,900 places of worship between them. As we have seen, these included obscure sects such as the Muggletonians, revivalist movements such as the Primitive Methodists and overseas churches such as the Moravians and the Huguenots. They also included major denominations such as the Baptists and the Congregationalists. Since 1851, many new denominations have been founded, for example the Salvation Army and the Pentecostalists. A vast array of new groupings arose in the last half of the twentieth century. Their history needs to be preserved, but they will not be considered here.

A comprehensive guide to the records of every denomination would take up a great deal of space and require a huge amount of research. The aim here is more basic. This book is intended to point the researcher in the direction of sources which are likely to record when Great Aunt Mary joined Shire Baptist Church and which will provide an overview of the life of that church. Family historians need to know where they can find evidence for their ancestors' lives. Local historians need to identify sources which reveal the life of the society they are researching. Sources likely to be useful to family historians are also usually important to local historians. Both need an appreciation of the way in which sources came into existence, both need to know where to find them and both need to know how to use them.

The prime focus here is on the sources. It is nevertheless true that local historians need to focus primarily on the questions that those sources might be able to answer. How many Nonconformists were there? Who were they? What influence did their churches have, both on their own members and on the wider community? What were the sociological differences between different Nonconformist congregations, and to what extent did they compete with each other? Were they predominantly middle class, or did they have the support of artisans? Did they involve themselves in political and social issues, for example trade unionism or Chartism? Did their advent destroy the unity of their local communities, as some Anglicans argued, or did they merely reflect pre-existing social and economic tensions? Did they operate in areas where there was inadequate Anglican provision, or did the Church of England prepare the way for them?

These are all questions which the local historian should ask. However, a prior knowledge of the sources that are available is necessary before they can be made to divulge their evidence. It is also important that Nonconformist historians should have an appreciation of denominational history in the wider historical context. General guides to sources are listed below, pp.30–4. For the wider context, see:

• Watts, Michael R. *The chapel and the nation: Nonconformity and the local historian*. Helps for students of history 97. (Historical Association, 1996).

See also:

• Hill, Christopher. 'History and denominational history', *Baptist Quarterly* 22, 1967–8, pp.65–71.

This book deals solely with sources specific to Nonconformists. Hence more general sources such as parish registers of baptisms, marriages and burials,[1] the decennial census[2] and probate records[3] are not dealt with here. Nor are published works such as the Oxford Dictionary of National Biography **www.oxforddnb.com**, or family history websites such as Genuki **www.genuki.org.uk**. If you are not already aware of such resources, read one of the many readily available general introductions to family and local history. The two most comprehensive works, which can be thoroughly recommended, are:

• Herber, Mark. *Ancestral Trails: the Complete Guide to British Genealogy and Family History*. (2nd ed. Sutton Publishing/Society of Genealogists, 2004).
• Hey, David, ed. *The Oxford Companion to Family and Local History*. (2nd ed. Oxford University Press, 2008).

Many general works of importance to the Nonconformist researcher are listed in:

• Raymond, Stuart A. *English Genealogy: a Bibliography*. (3rd ed. Federation of Family History Societies, 1996).

## THE INTERNET

Since the works just mentioned were published, there have been many developments on the internet. Numerous webpages provide indexes and transcripts of sources. More recently, the advent of the digital camera has allowed millions of sources to be digitized and reproduced by webmasters. It is vital to keep up to date with these developments.

A huge amount of information is available on the internet.[4] A useful directory of religious websites is provided by:

• Wabash Center: Religion on the Web
  **www.wabashcenter.wabash.edu/resources/guide_headings.aspx**

Much advice is available on the internet, but do be careful when using it. Institutional and official websites, such as those of the National Archives and Dr. Williams's Library, can generally be taken as authoritative. Many other websites are compiled by amateurs, some of whom are equally authoritative – but some are woeful. Family History Society sites may provide very useful information, but some are a lot better than others. The less authoritative may give themselves away by using terms incorrectly. For example, if a webpage uses the term 'parish records' when actually they mean 'parish registers of baptisms, marriages and burials' then you will know that the compiler does not realize that there are many parish records other than 'parish registers'.

Similarly, the terms 'transcript' and 'index' are frequently used incorrectly by the less informed. It is important to be aware of the difference between these two terms. An index is merely a list of terms, indicating where information relating to those terms can be found in the document being indexed. It does not necessarily tell you what that information is. A transcript is a more or less exact copy of a document made by a transcriber. Another related term which may cause confusion to the less initiated is 'calendar'. A calendar in this context is a summary of a document: more than just an index entry, but less than a full transcript, although it may record all the facts in the document. Indexes, calendars and transcripts may be found in manuscript, in printed books (frequently published by record societies or family history societies) and on the internet. Many are mentioned in this book.

Indexers, transcribers and calendar editors frequently make errors; it is not reasonable to expect absolute accuracy. Note that this applies to printed editions of original documents, just as much as it does to manuscripts and webpages. It is therefore always best, if possible, to consult the original document itself. However, the advent of digital cameras means that many digitized images of original documents are now available on the internet. These digitized images are normally accurate copies of the originals (unless the photographer misses a page!) and are a great boon to researchers. Some are on commercial sites which charge a fee for consultation. Others are free. The most important for the present purpose are the Nonconformist registers of baptisms, marriages and burials (see below, pp.59 69).

Many of the older books and journals mentioned in this book are also available on the internet. Some are available on denominational sites; these are noted in the appropriate place below. A number of sites specialize in digitizing books and it is always worth checking them before visiting libraries or buying older books from Amazon or other booksellers. They include (amongst others):

- The Internet Archive
  **www.archive.org**
- Hathi Trust Digital Library
  **http://babel.hathitrust.org**
- The Open Library
  **https://openlibrary.org**

For digitized Welsh journals, visit:

- Welsh Journals Online
  **http://welshjournals.llgc.org.uk**

For publications issued prior to 1800, the *English Short Title Catalogue* provides a comprehensive catalogue of all publications, with locations. The writings of many Nonconformist authors are included in:

- English Short Title Catalogue
  **http://estc.bl.uk**

Most of the books listed here can be located by using union catalogues listing the holdings of academic and public libraries. See:

- COPAC
  **http://copac.jisc.ac.uk**
- OCLC WorldCat
  **www.worldcat.org**

Digitized images of over 350,000 pre-1900 publications are available on three subscription databases: Early English Books Online, Eighteenth Century Collections Online and the British Library's

Nineteenth Century Collection. If you have access to these databases through your library, you can access all of them through:

- Historical Texts
  **http://historicaltexts.jisc.ac.uk**

Digitized images of many eighteenth-century books are available for free at:

- Eighteenth Century Collections Online: Text Creation Partnership
  **http://quod.lib.umich.edu/e/ecco**

### RECORD OFFICES AND LIBRARIES
Nonconformist records are held in a wide variety of record offices and libraries and it is important for researchers to be aware of them. Many of these institutions specialize in specific denominations and are discussed in subsequent chapters. Others have a much broader range. For a list of record offices, visit:

- Find an Archive in the UK and Beyond
  **http://discovery.nationalarchives.gov.uk/find-an-archive**

Archives held in many record offices are listed in a number of important union catalogues. The holdings of county record offices are catalogued in:

- The National Archives Discovery catalogue
  **http://discovery.nationalarchives.gov.uk**

For archives held by colleges and universities, see:

- Archives Hub
  **www.archiveshub.ac.uk**

Archives in London repositories are listed in:

- AIM 25
  **www.aim25.ac.uk**

For Wales, see:

- Archives Wales
  **www.archivesnetworkwales.info**

There are a number of libraries and record offices which specialize in Nonconformist books and archives. These are listed in:

- ABTAPL Theological and Religious Studies Directory
  **www.newman.ac.uk/abtapl/database/contents.html**
- Religious Archives Group. Religious Archives Directory
  **http://religiousarchivesgroup.org.uk/advice/directory**

A full list is also given in Field's 'Preserving Zion' (see below, p.75). For information on denominational history societies and libraries, see:

- Association of Denominational Historical Societies and Cognate Libraries
  **www.adhscl.org.uk**

In most counties there are historical/archaeological society libraries and/or private subscription libraries. There are too many to list them here, but they should be sought out. For example, both the Devon and Exeter Institution in Exeter and the Morrab Library in Penzance have extensive collections of local eighteenth- and nineteenth-century newspapers. The Wiltshire Archaeological and Natural History Society holds a range of Wiltshire Nonconformist ephemera. Local history societies, some of which have libraries, are listed by:

- Local History Online: Directory of Local History and Allied Societies
  **www.local-history.co.uk/Groups/index.html**

For independent libraries, see:

- Association of Independent Libraries
  **http://independentlibraries.co.uk/**

Relevant sources are sometimes also held by local Family History Society libraries; Devon Family History Society, for example, has extensive Methodist holdings, including a collection of Methodist circuit plans. Family History Societies are listed on the Federation of Family History Societies' website **www.ffhs.org.uk**.

**The Major Repositories**
Brief details of the major repositories holding Nonconformist records from various different denominations are noted here. More information on their denominational holdings is given in succeeding chapters.

**The National Archives** holds the archives of central government, which include a number of collections of importance to Nonconformist researchers. They include documents such as the state papers (the correspondence of the secretaries of state, which are extremely wide-ranging), recusant rolls, which record fines imposed on those who failed to attend their parish church, various oath rolls recording Nonconformists who swore loyalty to the Crown, meeting house licences permitting premises to be used for Nonconformist worship, Nonconformist registers of baptisms, marriages and burials collected by the Registrar General when civil registration was introduced and the 1851 religious census. These are all discussed in detail below; however, for an overview, visit:

- How to look for records of Nonconformists
  **www.nationalarchives.gov.uk/help-with-your-research/research-guides/Nonconformists**

Other research guides on the National Archives website may also be useful. For an overall guide to its holdings, see:

- Bevan, Amanda. *Tracing your Ancestors in the National Archives*. (7th ed. National Archives, 2003).

More detailed information on specific records is available at:

- National Archives Discovery Catalogue
  **http://discovery.nationalarchives.gov.uk**

*The National Archives at Kew.*

**Dr. Williams's Library** holds extensive collections of letters and papers, various surveys of Nonconformist churches, the records of a number of denominational organizations, funeral sermons and many books. Its particular strength is the old Dissent, especially Congregational and Presbyterian, although it does have material relating to Baptists, Methodists and other denominations. Amongst its holdings are the records of the Westminster Assembly of Divines (1643–52), which failed in its attempt to replace the established church with a Presbyterian structure of church government.[5] It also holds the records of many Dissenting congregations, mostly from London and the Home Counties. Details can be found at:

• Dr. Williams Trust and Library; Congregational Library
  **www.dwlib.co.uk**

See also:

- Creasey, John Oliver. *Dr. Williams's Library : the last fifty years.* (Dr Williams's Trust, 2000).
- Payne, Ernest Alexander. *A venerable Dissenting institution: Dr. Williams's Library, 1729-1979.* (Dr. Williams' Trust, 1979).
- Twinn, Kenneth. *Dr. Williams's Library: Guide to the Manuscripts.* (Dr. Williams's Trust, 1969).
- Twinn, Kenneth. 'Sources for church history 2: Dr. Williams' Library', *Local Historian* 9, 1970–1, pp.115–20.

The holdings of this library are catalogued in:

- Dr. Williams's Library. *Catalogue of the library ... founded pursuant to the will of the Rev. Daniel Williams / Dr. Williams's Library.* (2 vols. 1841). There are a number of subsequent volumes. However, over 40,000 books, plus some 67,000 journal articles, have now been catalogued online, at **http://dwlib.co.uk/catalogue**, increasingly rendering these volumes redundant.

A chronological catalogue of early books (including many sermons) is also provided by:

- *Early Nonconformity, 1566-1800: a catalogue of books in Dr. Williams's Library, London.* 12 vols. (G. K. Hall, 1968).

**The John Rylands University Library of Manchester** is renowned for its Methodist archives (see Chapter 5), but it also holds much material relevant to other denominations. This includes many local histories, biographies, hymn books and sermons. It also includes the correspondence of many ministers and laymen and the archives of a variety of training institutions and other denominational organizations, for example the minutes of Manchester Unitarian Sunday School Union, 1864–1914. The archives of a small number of individual congregations are held. Particularly important collections include those of the Unitarian College Manchester, the Northern Baptist College, and Lancashire Independent or Northern

College. There are also substantial collections relating to the Christian Brethren, the Moravians and the Quakers. Much information (including a catalogue) is provided on the library's website:

- John Rylands University Library of Manchester Special Collections **www.library.manchester.ac.uk/search-resources/guide-to-special-collections**

The Rylands' collection is also catalogued on:

- The National Archives Discovery catalogue **http://discovery.nationalarchives.gov.uk**

For more information, see:

- Field, Clive D. 'Sources for the Study of Protestant Nonconformity in the John Rylands University Library of Manchester', *Bulletin of the John Rylands University Library of Manchester*, 71(2), 1989, pp.103–39.
- Field, Clive D. *Theology and Church History: a guide to research resources*. (John Rylands University Library of Manchester, 1990).
- 'Christian theology and ecclesiastical history', *Bulletin of the John Rylands University Library of Manchester* 80(2), 1998, pp.65–99.
- *A guide to special collections of the John Rylands University Library of Manchester*. (1999). This includes a chapter on 'Christian theology and ecclesiastical history'.

**The Borthwick Institute for Archives** in York **www.york.ac.uk/borthwick** holds much material relating to Dissent in Northern England. For details, see:

- Sheils, William. 'Sources for the history of Dissent and Catholicism at the Borthwick Institute', *Borthwick Institute Bulletin* 3(1), 1983, pp.11–28.

**Harris Manchester College Library** in Oxford holds another major collection of Dissenting literature. As well as its books, it has a substantial collection of ephemera, such as chapel histories, hymn books and Sunday school literature. It also holds the papers of many prominent Unitarians. Its manuscripts are listed in:

• Porter, Dennis. *A catalogue of the manuscripts in Harris Manchester College, Oxford.* (1998).

An updated version of this catalogue is available at:

• Harris Manchester College Oxford: College Library
  **www.hmc.ox.ac.uk**
  Click 'Library & Archives' and 'Archives and Library History'.

**The National Library of Wales www.llgc.org.uk** holds the archives of the Presbyterian Church of Wales (or Welsh Calvinistic Methodists), the Welsh Wesleyan Assembly and the Congregational Federation of Wales, together with many Welsh Baptist chapel records. These are listed in its online archives and manuscript catalogues. Many chapel records are also held in Welsh local record offices. They are listed by:

• Archives Wales
  **www.archivesnetworkwales.info**

### EARLY NONCONFORMIST RECORDS

Most Nonconformist records date from the Great Ejection, although Quaker records commence during the Interregnum and many records of Elizabethan Huguenots are available. The great bulk of the evidence for separatists before the Civil War derive from the efforts of church and state to drive them out of existence. The Family of Love is discussed below (see p.215). Court records from both secular and ecclesiastical courts provide useful information. Much was published in:

- Burrage, Champlin. *The Early English Dissenters in the Light of Recent Research (1550-1641).* (2 vols. Cambridge University Press, 1912).

Some of the English colonies in North America owe their origin to English separatists, such as the Pilgrim Fathers. There are many lists of early emigrants, many of whom were puritans. For a bibliography of listings, see:

- Filby, P.W. *Passenger and immigration lists bibliography 1538-1900, being a guide to published lists of arrivals in the United States and Canada.* (2nd ed. Gale, 1988).

The outbreak of civil war in 1642 opened the floodgates to a ferment of ideas and also to the publication of the earliest English

*The Pilgrim Fathers' ship* Mayflower.

newspapers. The literature preserved in the British Library's Thomason tracts includes a huge amount of information on religious activity in England, as well as the earliest news sheets. This collection is described by:

- Thomason Collection of Civil War Tracts
  **www.bl.uk/reshelp/findhelprestype/prbooks/thomason/ thomasoncivilwar.html**

The tracts are catalogued in the British Library's online catalogue. There is also a printed catalogue:

- *Catalogue of the pamphlets, books, newspapers and manuscripts relating to the Civil War, Commonwealth and Restoration, collected by George Thomason, 1640-1661.* (London, 1908; reprinted Ann Arbor, 1977).

The collection has been digitized in the Early English Books Online database (see above, pp.27–8). The collection is also available on microfilm in many libraries:

- *Thomason tracts, 1640-1660.* 256 microfilm reels. (University Microfilms International, 1977–81).

A particularly valuable, if prejudiced, commentary on the 'sectaries' of the period, which draws on information from many localities, is provided by:

- Edwards, Thomas. *Gangraena.* (The Rota, University of Exeter, 1977). This was originally published in 1646, sub-titled as *A catalogue and discovery of many of the errours, heresies, blasphemies and pernicious practices of the sectaries of this time, vented and acted in England in these four last years, as also, a particular narration of divers stories, remarkable passages, letters; an extract of many letters, all concerning the present sects.*

## BIOGRAPHICAL DICTIONARIES OF NONCONFORMISTS

The great majority of the ministers ejected in 1662 were Presbyterians, although there were c.200 Independents and 19 Baptists. Brief details of 1,760 clergy lives are given in:

• Matthews, A.G. *Calamy revised, being a revision of Edmund Calamy's Account of the ministers and others ejected and silenced, 1660-2.* (Clarendon Press, 1934). Calamy's original work, published in 1713–27, should also be consulted.

For Wales, see:

• Jones, R.T., & Owens, B.G. 'Anghydffurfwyr Cymru, 1660-2', *Y Cofiadur* 32, 1962, pp. 3–93.

A more detailed regional survey is provided by:

• Nightingale, B. *The ejected of 1662 in Cumberland & Westmorland: their predecessors and successors.* 2 vols. (Manchester University Press, 1911).

There are a number of other biographical dictionaries of ministers and churchmen. Most relate to specific denominations and are noted in the denominational chapters below. A broader remit, featuring over 3,500 evangelicals, is taken by:

• Lewis, Donald M., ed. *The Blackwell Dictionary of Evangelical Biography 1730-1860.* 2 vols. (Blackwell Reference, 1995).

See also:

• Larsen, Timothy. *Biographical Dictionary of Evangelicals.* (Inter-Varsity Press, 2003).
• Pine, L.G. *Who's Who in the Free Churches (and other Denominations).* (Shaw Publishing, 1951).

Details of theological colleges (not just in Wales) attended by clergy of all denominations[6] are provided in:

• Theological Colleges attended by Welsh ministers and priests
  **www.genuki.org.uk/big/wal/ChurchHistory/TheoColl**

### GOVERNMENT SURVEYS

A number of surveys of Nonconformist strength have been undertaken by both church[7] and state. The Compton census was compiled by bishops in 1676. This is a head-count of conformists, papists and Nonconformists in each parish. A very few name-lists have also survived. Some Compton returns are printed by Turner (see p.44). A full transcription of the principal manuscripts (excluding the name-lists) is provided by:

• Whiteman, Anne, ed. *The Compton Census of 1676: a critical edition.* Records of social and economic history new series 10. (Oxford University Press, 1986).

Less attention has been paid to the returns of Nonconformist places of worship which were called for by a resolution of the House of Commons in 1829. These were destroyed by fire in 1834, but the return for Lancashire had been published, and copies of other returns had been retained amongst Quarter Sessions records, where they can sometimes still be found. Returns list places of worship and their denominations and may include numbers and comments from incumbents. A detailed discussion is provided in:

• Ambler, R.W. 'A lost source? The 1829 returns of non-Anglican places of worship', *Local Historian* 17(8), 1987, pp.483–9.

See also:

• Caplan, N. 'Religious Dissent in Sussex, c.1829', *Journal of the United Reformed Church History Society* 1, 1973, pp.197–203.
• Tranter, Margery. 'Many and diverse Dissenters: the 1829 returns for Derbyshire', *Local Historian* 18(4), 1988, pp.162–7.

More comprehensive coverage is provided by the religious census of 1851, which documents the dramatic expansion of Nonconformity in the early nineteenth century. It shows that there were ten times as many congregations in 1851 as there had been in 1773.[8] It also shows that the number of Nonconformist chapels exceeded the number of Anglican churches. The census covers all places of worship. Its published reports give total numbers of places of worship and attenders in each of 624 registration districts. For two digitized reproductions online, visit:

• British Religion in Numbers: Religious Census 1851 Online
  **www.brin.ac.uk/2010/religious-census-1851-online**

The original returns, held by The National Archives (class HO 129), provide information on each individual place of worship, including the numbers attending all services on 30 March 1851, the number of free seats available, the dates chapels were erected and other comments from incumbents. Returns might be signed by ministers or church officers; the latter sometimes indicated their occupations. A detailed study is provided by:

• Snell, K.D.M., & Ell, Paul S. *Rival Jerusalems: the geography of Victorian religion*. (Cambridge University Press, 2000).

See also:

• Ambler, R.W. 'The 1851 census of religious worship', *Local Historian* 11(7), 1975, pp.375–81.
• Thompson, David M. 'The religious census of 1851', in Lawton, Richard, ed. *The Census and Social Structure: an Interpretative Guide to Nineteenth Century Censuses for England and Wales*. (Frank Cass, 1978), pp.241–88.

For a detailed analysis of one county's returns, see:

• Wolffe, J. *The Religious Census of 1851 in Yorkshire*. (Borthwick Papers, 108, 2005).

TABLE F.—*continued.*

### NEWCASTLE-ON-TYNE (Municipal Borough). Population, 87,784. — NEWPORT (Municipal Borough). Population, 19,323.

| RELIGIOUS DENOMINATION. | No. of Places of Worship | Sittings Free | Sittings Appro-priated | Sittings Total | Attend. Morning | Attend. After-noon | Attend. Evening | No. of Places of Worship | Sittings Free | Sittings Appro-priated | Sittings Total | Attend. Morning | Attend. After-noon | Attend. Evening |
|---|---|---|---|---|---|---|---|---|---|---|---|---|---|---|
| TOTAL | 51 | 11,165 | 15,931 | 23,806 | 18,710 | 4640 | 11,730 | 21 | 4635 | 5383 | 10,018 | 5365 | 646 | 5424 |
| **PROTESTANT CHURCHES:** | | | | | | | | | | | | | | |
| Church of England | 11 | 2877 | 7051 | 9928 | 7202 | 2643 | 4891 | 3 | 905 | 631 | 1536 | 1177 | 128 | 820 |
| Church of Scotland | 2 | 500 | .. | 1500 | 625 | .. | 800 | .. | .. | .. | .. | .. | .. | .. |
| United Presby. Church | 3 | 500 | .. | 1200 | 1170 | 225 | 275 | .. | .. | .. | .. | .. | .. | .. |
| Presby. Ch. in England | 2 | 260 | 1310 | 1570 | 704 | .. | 548 | .. | .. | .. | .. | .. | .. | .. |
| Independents | 2 | 86 | 950 | 1036 | 826 | .. | 518 | 5 | 755 | 1068 | 1823 | 873 | .. | 1007 |
| Particular Baptists | 5 | 1548 | 350 | 1898 | 1028 | 40 | 698 | 3 | 1000 | 924 | 1924 | 912 | .. | 1150 |
| Scotch Baptists | 1 | 250 | .. | 250 | 44 | .. | 42 | .. | .. | .. | .. | .. | .. | .. |
| Baptists (*not otherwise defined*) | | | | | | | | | | | | | | |
| Society of Friends | 1 | 512 | .. | 512 | 217 | 112 | .. | .. | .. | .. | .. | .. | .. | .. |
| Unitarians | 2 | 257 | 815 | 1072 | 461 | .. | 118 | .. | .. | .. | .. | .. | .. | .. |
| Wesleyan Methodists | 6 | 1150 | 2502 | 3652 | 1270 | 139 | 1307 | 2 | 590 | 1250 | 1840 | 463 | .. | 634 |
| Methodist New Connex. | 3 | 680 | 782 | 1472 | 210 | 145 | 280 | .. | .. | .. | .. | .. | .. | .. |
| Primitive Methodists | 4 | 1066 | 757 | 1823 | 806 | 370 | 742 | .. | .. | .. | .. | .. | .. | .. |
| Bible Christians | .. | .. | .. | .. | .. | .. | .. | 1 | 50 | 180 | 230 | 71 | .. | 84 |
| Wesleyan Association | .. | .. | .. | .. | .. | .. | .. | .. | .. | .. | .. | .. | .. | .. |
| Wesleyan Reformers | 2 | 495 | .. | 495 | 630 | .. | 780 | 2 | 425 | 250 | 675 | 210 | .. | 409 |
| Welsh Calv. Methodists | .. | .. | .. | .. | .. | .. | .. | 1 | 150 | 80 | 230 | 260 | 98 | 201 |
| New Church | 1 | 350 | 50 | 400 | 70 | .. | 70 | .. | .. | .. | .. | .. | .. | .. |
| Isolated Congregations | 2 | 150 | .. | 150 | 8 | 66 | 57 | 2 | 460 | .. | 460 | 19 | 20 | 19 |
| **OTHER CHRISTIAN CHS.:** | | | | | | | | | | | | | | |
| Roman Catholics | 2 | 410 | 1334 | 1744 | 3389 | 900 | 604 | 1 | 300 | 1000 | 1300 | 1300 | 200 | 700 |
| Latter Day Saints | .. | .. | .. | .. | .. | .. | .. | 1 | .. | .. | .. | 60 | 200 | 400 |
| Jews | 1 | 74 | 30 | 104 | 50 | .. | .. | .. | .. | .. | .. | .. | .. | .. |

### NORTHAMPTON (Municipal Borough). Population, 26,657. — NORWICH (Municipal Borough). Population, 68,195.

| RELIGIOUS DENOMINATION. | No. of Places of Worship | Sittings Free | Sittings Appro-priated | Sittings Total | Attend. Morning | Attend. After-noon | Attend. Evening | No. of Places of Worship | Sittings Free | Sittings Appro-priated | Sittings Total | Attend. Morning | Attend. After-noon | Attend. Evening |
|---|---|---|---|---|---|---|---|---|---|---|---|---|---|---|
| TOTAL | 28 | 5049 | 7622 | 14,268 | 7381 | 2226 | 7289 | 86 | 9422 | 10,330 | 28,834 | 13,240 | 10,274 | 7908 |
| **PROTESTANT CHURCHES:** | | | | | | | | | | | | | | |
| Church of England | 11 | 2407 | 3436 | 6840 | 2987 | 1031 | 2513 | 41 | 8986 | 2533 | 15,551 | 6520 | 6381 | 2186 |
| Independents | 3 | 339 | 1467 | 1806 | 1518 | .. | 987 | 3 | 380 | 1866 | 2246 | 1785 | 250 | 989 |
| Particular Baptists | 5 | 580 | 1241 | 2121 | 1545 | 675 | 1495 | 4 | 699 | 1748 | 2447 | 1639 | 817 | 1169 |
| General Baptists, New Connexion | .. | .. | .. | .. | .. | .. | .. | 1 | 150 | 150 | 300 | 200 | 150 | 150 |
| Baptists (*not otherwise defined*) | .. | .. | .. | .. | .. | .. | .. | 3 | 206 | .. | 256 | 116 | 138 | 132 |
| Society of Friends | 1 | 400 | .. | 400 | 59 | .. | 450 | 1 | 408 | .. | 408 | 93 | 41 | .. |
| Unitarians | 1 | 95 | 195 | 290 | 230 | .. | 160 | 1 | 120 | 380 | 500 | 401 | .. | 136 |
| Wesleyan Methodists | 2 | 465 | 932 | 1397 | 796 | 388 | 1236 | 5 | 696 | 1495 | 2191 | 494 | 506 | 669 |
| Primitive Methodists | 1 | 128 | 172 | 300 | 79 | 92 | 128 | 4 | 196 | 858 | 1054 | 607 | 604 | 788 |
| Wesleyan Association | 1 | 35 | 179 | 214 | 107 | .. | 120 | .. | .. | .. | .. | .. | .. | .. |
| Wesleyan Reformers | .. | .. | .. | .. | .. | .. | .. | 1 | 120 | 450 | 570 | 322 | 117 | 294 |
| L'Huntingdon's Connex. | .. | .. | .. | .. | .. | .. | .. | 1 | 250 | 700 | 950 | 160 | 115 | 80 |
| New Church | .. | .. | .. | .. | .. | .. | .. | 1 | 12 | 120 | 132 | 90 | .. | 106 |
| Isolated Congregations | 1 | 200 | .. | 200 | 30 | 40 | 100 | 11 | 1740 | .. | 1740 | 407 | 974 | 1035 |
| **OTHER CHRISTIAN CHS.:** | | | | | | | | | | | | | | |
| Roman Catholics | 1 | .. | .. | 300 | .. | .. | .. | 1 | .. | .. | .. | 250 | .. | .. |
| Latter Day Saints | 1 | 400 | .. | 400 | 30 | .. | 100 | 1 | 400 | .. | 400 | .. | 181 | 150 |
| Jews | .. | .. | .. | .. | .. | .. | .. | 1 | 59 | 30 | 89 | 26 | .. | 24 |

NEWCASTLE-ON-TYNE.—The returns omit to state the number of *sittings* in one place of worship belonging to the UNITED PRESBYTERIAN CHURCH, attended by a maximum number of 275 persons at a service; and in one place belonging to an ISOLATED CONGREGATION, attended by a maximum number of 30 persons at a service.—The number of *attendants* is not given for one place of worship belonging to the ESTABLISHED CHURCH.—Neither *sittings* nor *attendants* are given for one place of worship belonging to the PARTICULAR BAPTISTS; and for one place belonging to the BAPTISTS, not otherwise defined.

NEWPORT.—The returns omit to state the number of *sittings* in one place of worship belonging to the ESTABLISHED CHURCH, attended by a maximum number of 200 persons at a service; and in one place belonging to the LATTER DAY SAINTS, attended by a maximum number of 400 persons at a service.

NORTHAMPTON.—The number of *attendants* is not given for one place of worship belonging to the ESTABLISHED CHURCH and for one place belonging to the ROMAN CATHOLICS.

NORWICH.—The returns omit to state the number of *sittings* in three places of worship belonging to the ESTABLISHED CHURCH, attended by a maximum number of 380 persons at a service; in one place belonging to the PRIMITIVE METHODISTS, attended by a maximum number of 15 persons at a service; in one place belonging to an ISOLATED CONGREGATION, attended by a maximum number of 59 persons at a service; and in one place belonging to the ROMAN CATHOLICS, attended by a maximum number of 250 persons at a service.—The number of *attendants* is not given for one place of worship belonging to the ESTABLISHED CHURCH.—Neither *sittings* nor *attendants* are given for one place of worship belonging to an ISOLATED CONGREGATION.

*A return from the 1851 Religious Census.*

Returns for some counties have been published. See, for example:

- Jones, Ieuan Gwynedd, & Williams, David, eds. *The Religious Census of 1851, a calendar of the returns relating to Wales*. (2 vols. University of Wales Press, 1976–81).
- Timmins, T.C.B., ed. *Suffolk Returns from the Census of Religious Worship 1851*. (Suffolk Record Society, 39, 1997).
- Ward, Graham S., ed. *The 1851 Religious Census of Northamptonshire*. Victor Hatley memorial volume 2. (Northamptonshire Record Society, 2007).
- Wolffe, J. ed. *Yorkshire. Returns of the 1851 Census of Religious Worship*. Vol. 1: *Introduction, City of York and East Riding*; Vol. 2: *West Riding (North)*; Vol. 3: *West Riding (South)*. (Borthwick Texts and Studies 25, 31 & 32, 2000–5).

Many other relevant publications are listed in:

- Field, Clive D. 'The 1851 religious census of Great Britain: a bibliographical guide for local and regional historians', *Local Historian* 27(4), 1997, pp.194–217. This can be downloaded at **www.balh.org.uk/publications/local-historian**.

### OTHER SURVEYS
A statistical survey conducted by newspapers is reported in:

- Mearns, Andrew. *The statistics of attendance at public worship, as published in England, Wales and Scotland by the local press between October, 1881 and February, 1882, tabulated*. (Hodder & Stoughton, 1882).

Some twentieth-century statistics are presented in:

- *Prospects for the eighties: from a census of the churches in 1979 / undertaken by the Nationwide Initiative in Evangelism*. 2 vols. (Bible Society, 1980).
- Brierley, P. W. *Christian England: what the 1989 English Church census reveals*. (MARC Europe, 1991).

• Brierley, P. W. *Churchgoers in England, district by district: based on the results of the 1989 English Church Census.* (Challenge 2000/Christian Research, 1990).
• Brierley, P.W. *Prospects for the nineties: trends and tables from the English church census, with denominations and churchmanships.* (MARC Europe, 1991).

For London, more detailed information is given in two surveys conducted by newspapers:

• *The religious census of London.* (Hodder & Stoughton, 1888. Reprinted from the *British Weekly*).
• Mudie-Smith, Richard, ed. *The Religious Life of London.* (Hodder & Stoughton, 1904).

Statistics of attendance at Welsh Nonconformist churches can be found in the appendices of:

• *Report of the Royal Commission on the Church of England and other religious bodies in Wales and Monmouthshire.* (8 vols. in 9. Parliamentary Papers 1910, XIV–XIX. Cd.5437. 1910–11). Appendices are in vols. XVIII & XIX.

See also:

• Brierley, Peter W. *Prospects for Wales: report of the 1982 census of the Churches.* (Bible Society, 1983).

Statistical and other documents from all denominations are available in a microfilm edition:

• *The state of the churches in Great Britain and Ireland 1974, as shown in their own official yearbooks and other reports.* (1 microfilm reels. Ecumenism Research Agency, [1975]).

An overall view of nineteenth- and twentieth-century attendance statistics is provided by:

• Gill, Robin. *The Empty Church Revisited*. (2nd ed. Ashgate, 2003).

Although its focus is primarily on contemporary religion, some useful information is provided by:

• British Religion in Numbers
  **www.brin.ac.uk**

## GOVERNMENT SOURCES

One of the tasks of the Nonconformist local historian is to trace how the numbers recorded in the Compton census of 1676 increased to the numbers revealed in 1851. There are a wide variety of sources which can be examined for evidence of this process. Many of these sources relate to specific denominations and will be discussed in the relevant chapters below. Others cross denominational boundaries. Most of those compiled for the government and the Church of England are in this category. There is extensive evidence relating to Nonconformists in The National Archives, as has already been seen. Quarter Sessions and diocesan records, held by local record offices, also contain much information.

### State Papers

The State Papers, now in The National Archives, are probably the most important source for English history in the sixteenth and seventeenth centuries. They are a general record of the proceedings of government and deal with a wide range of topics. They contain much valuable information about Nonconformity. The *Calendars of State Papers* are widely available in libraries; details of those for the late Stuart period are given in:

• Home Affairs in the Early Modern Period: State Papers Domestic 1547–1649
  **www.nationalarchives.gov.uk/help-with-your-research/
  research-guides/state-papers-domestic-1547-1649/**
  Similar pages are available for 1642–60, 1660–1714 and 1714–82.

In 1672, Charles II issued his Declaration of Indulgence. Under it, Nonconformist ministers could apply for licences to teach their congregations and buildings could be licensed for Nonconformist worship. The State Papers include these licences. They can be found in classes SP 29/320-1, SP 44/27 and SP 44/33A-B, and are printed, together with a number of seventeenth-century episcopal surveys of Nonconformist strength, in:

• Turner, G.L., ed. *Original Records of Early Nonconformity under Persecution and Indulgence*. (3 vols. T. Fisher Unwin, 1911).

See also:

• Nuttall, Geoffrey F., ed. 'Lyon Turner's Original records: notes and identifications', *Transactions of the Congregational Historical Society*, 14, 1940–4, pp.14–24, 112–20 & 181–7; 15, 1945–8, pp.41–7; 19, 1960–4, pp.160–4.

The names of licensed preachers and of their places of worship, are also given in an appendix to:

• Bate, Frank. *The Declaration of Indulgence: a study in the rise of organized Dissent*. Liverpool University Press, 1908.

### Recusant Rolls

Between 1592 and 1691, those who failed to attend their parish church were liable to substantial fines. Fines were imposed by Quarter Sessions (see below, pp.48–9). Estreats were sent to the Exchequer, which recorded them in the recusant rolls and instructed sheriffs to collect the fines. The majority of those fined were Roman Catholics; however, many Nonconformists also suffered, especially after the Restoration and during the Exclusion crisis of the early 1680s. In 1679, 70 per cent of those charged with recusancy in Middlesex were Catholics; the number dropped to 6 per cent in 1683.[9] The recusant rolls are in The National Archives, classes E 376-7 (see also E 351 and E 370). A number have been published by the Catholic Record Society. For a useful introduction, see:

• Bowler, Hugh, ed. *Recusant roll no.2 (1593-1594)*. (Catholic Record Society 57, 1965).

## Meeting House Licences and Surveys

Meeting house licences were re-introduced in 1689. They identify the places where Nonconformists met, with the names of those who applied for them. They were issued by bishops, quarter sessions and archdeacons. Petitions for, and registers of, these licences are to be found in county record offices. They are described in:

- Welch, Edwin. 'The registration of meeting houses', *Journal of the Society of Archivists* 3, 1966, pp.116–20.

The information provided by these records does not necessarily include denominational allegiances. Methodists in particular were prone to describe themselves as 'Protestant' or 'Independent'. A number of collections of meeting house licences have been published. Useful introductions are printed in the following:

## Bedfordshire
- Welch, Edwin, ed. *Bedfordshire chapels and meeting houses: official registration, 1672-1901.* (Publications of the Bedfordshire Historical Record Society 75, 1996).

## Berkshire
- Spurrier, Lisa, ed. *Berkshire Nonconformist Meeting House Registrations, 1689-1852.* (2 vols. Berkshire Record Society, 9–10, 2005).

## Staffordshire
- Donaldson, Barbara, ed. *The Registrations of Dissenting chapels and meeting houses in Staffordshire 1689-1852: extracted from the return in the General Register Office made under the Protestant Dissenters Act of 1852 (15 and 16 Vic. c.36).* (Collections for a History of Staffordshire 4th series 3, Staffordshire Record Society, 1960).

## Wiltshire
- Chandler, J.H., ed. *Wiltshire Dissenters' meeting house certificates and registrations 1689-1852.* (Wiltshire Record Society 40, 1985).

This licensing system was replaced by the Registrar-General's 'Worship Register' in 1852. He required a return from all former licensing authorities of meeting houses licensed since 1689. These returns are now in The National Archives, class RG 31. They duplicate the registers already mentioned, but may be useful if the latter have been lost. The Worship Register is ongoing. It is described in:

- Rose, R.B. 'Some national sources for protestant Nonconformist and Roman Catholic history', *Bulletin of the Institute of Historical Research* 31, 1958, pp.79–83.

Staffordshire returns to the Registrar-General have been published:

- Donaldson, Barbara, ed. *The Registrations of Dissenting chapels and meeting houses in Staffordshire 1689-1852: extracted from the return in the General Register Office made under the Protestant Dissenters Act of 1852 (15 and 16 Vic. c.36).* (Collections for a History of Staffordshire 4th series 3. Staffordshire Record Society, 1960).

Certificates of registration since 1852 are in The National Archives, class RG 70. Registrations have been published in the *London Gazette* **www.thegazette.co.uk** and also, at irregular intervals, in the Registrar General's *Official List* . . . .

The 1852 returns for Bedfordshire have been collated with the original ecclesiastical and Quarter Sessions records and published together with subsequent entries in the Worship Register:

- Welch, Edwin, ed. *Bedfordshire chapels and meeting houses: official registration, 1672-1901.* (Publications of the Bedfordshire Historical Record Society 75, 1996).

There are also a number of official returns listing chapels and meeting houses in the Parliamentary papers.[10] These include:

- *A Return of the number of registered Dissenting meeting houses and Roman Catholic chapels in England and Wales.* Parliamentary Paper 1836 (443) XL. Lists numbers in each county and town, with some additional information.
- *List of returns to Registrar General of number of certified places of religious worship of protestant Dissenters.* Parliamentary paper 1852–3 (156) LXXVIII.
- *Return of churches chapels and buildings registered for religious worship in the registration districts of Great Britain, showing the religious denomination to which such churches, chapels and buildings belong.* Parliamentary papers series, 1882, L. Lists churches registered in 1856 and 1876.

### Nonconformist Trust Deeds

Chapel building necessarily involved the purchase of land in trust. Trust deeds normally survive amongst church archives and offer a great deal of information about congregations, their lands and buildings, their doctrinal beliefs and their organization, as well as the names of trustees. Trustees were important: they were responsible for the maintenance of chapels. They also controlled who could use them. Those who wished to secede from a particular denomination needed the support of chapel trustees, otherwise, they lost the use of their chapel. Trust deeds frequently included a statement of doctrine, intended to prevent seceders having the use of chapels. The importance of such deeds was illustrated when Presbyterian churches became Unitarian. The Unitarians had to secure the passage of the Dissenters' Chapels Act, 1844 (see below, p.83) to secure possession of their buildings.

In the eighteenth century, the Methodists were the first to develop model deeds which could be used for all their chapels. They also developed the deed poll, which gave the denominational leadership trusteeship powers over all their chapels (see below, p.164). The Methodist lead was subsequently followed by the Salvation Army and by some other denominations.

Between 1736 and 1890, some 40,000 Nonconformist trust deeds were enrolled on the Close rolls (The National Archives, class C54). Enrolments are described in:

- Ambler, R.W. 'Enrolled trust deeds: a source for the history of nineteenth-century Nonconformity', *Archives* 20(90), 1993, pp.177–86.

See also:

- Welch, Edwin. 'Nonconformist trust deeds', *Journal of the Society of Archivists* 3, 1968, pp.397–403.

## Quarter Sessions Records

The records of Quarter Sessions include a number of sources relating to Nonconformists. Meeting House licences have already been mentioned. Fines for non-attendance at church, imposed at Quarter Sessions, were the basis of recusant rolls. Presentments for holding conventicles may also be found. Convictions were entered in Quarter Sessions order books.

Presentments and fines indicate hostility towards Nonconformity, not its prevalence. Their absence does not mean there were no Nonconformists. Churchwardens could be sympathetic to Nonconformity, or even active Nonconformists themselves. If so, they avoided making presentments. Presentments for holding conventicles may not be very informative; they frequently indicate neither denominations, nor the numbers attending. As we have seen, penal legislation against Nonconformists was repealed after 1688, although various disabilities remained.

Quarter Sessions order books might also record penalties against Quakers which other Dissenters avoided. Quakers refused to take oaths, which were required in court proceedings. They were punished for doing so until legislation of 1723, which enabled them to affirm their loyalty, rather than taking an oath. Affirmation rolls can be found amongst Quarter Sessions records. They continued, however, to refuse payment of tithes and church rates and were frequently distrained as a result.

A useful chapter on 'religion' in Quarter Sessions records is included in:

• Raymond, Stuart A. *Tracing your Ancestors in County Records: a Guide for Family and Local Historians*. (Pen & Sword, 2016), pp.11–20.

Introductions to published Quarter Sessions records sometimes include useful information on Nonconformity. See, for example:

• Peyton, S.A., ed. *Minutes of proceedings in Quarter Sessions held for the Parts of Kesteven in the County of Lincoln, 1674-1695*. Vol.1. Lincoln Record Society 25, 1931.

## DIOCESAN ARCHIVES

Much information about Nonconformists can be found in diocesan archives, which are normally deposited in local record offices. Visitation records can be particular useful. Bishops were supposed to conduct regular visitations of their dioceses. One of the topics they investigated was the prevalence of Nonconformity. The papers which derive from Bishop Fell's visitation of Oxford Diocese in 1682–3 are typical. They include letters from clergy identifying Nonconformists and a list of Dissenters. Edited with them is a return of 'conventicles' for 1669. See:

• Clapinson, Mary, ed. *Bishop Fell and Nonconformity: visitation documents from the Oxford Diocese, 1682-83*. (Oxfordshire Record Society 52, 1980).

Prior to visitations, bishops sometimes sent out preliminary queries to their clergy. These often sought information on Nonconformists. In 1821, for example, one of the questions Bishop Carey of Exeter, asked was: 'Have you any Papists or Dissenters? If the latter, of what kind or denomination? What teachers of each are there resident in your parish, or occasionally visiting it? Are they licensed? What places have they of public meeting, licensed or otherwise?' The answers such questions received obviously provide much valuable information about Dissent. Many 'replies to queries' have been published; see, for example:

- Broad, John, ed. *Bishop Wake's Summary of Visitation returns from the Diocese of Lincoln 1706-1715*. (2 vols. Records of Social and Economic History new series 49–50. Oxford University Press for the British Academy, 2012). Vol. 2 covers counties other than Lincolnshire.
- Cook, Michael, ed. *The Diocese of Exeter in 1821: Bishop Carey's replies to queries before visitation*. (2 vols. Devon & Cornwall Record Society, New series 3–4, 1958–60).
- Episcopal Visitation Returns, 1744 and 1779 [for Devon] **http://foda.org.uk/visitations/intro/introduction1.htm**
- Fisher, Howard, ed. *Church life in Georgian Nottinghamshire: Archbishop Drummond's Parish Visitation Returns 1764*. (Thoroton Society Record Series 46. 2012).

## CONTEMPORARY WRITINGS

More sympathetic information about Dissenters is to be found in their own autobiographies, letters, diaries, sermons and books. There are many of these and they frequently provide much valuable information about Nonconformist activities. The online catalogues described above (pp.27–8) can be used to identify these works. The writings of many Puritan authors can be found at:

- Fire and Ice: Puritan and Reformed Writings **www.Puritansermons.com/index.htm**

If your library has access (a subscription is required), then it may be worth consulting:

- The Digital Library of Classic Protestant Texts **http://alexanderstreet.com/products/digital-library-classic-protestant-texts**

All local historians interested in the late seventeenth century should check the lives, letters and journals of the Nonconformist preacher, Richard Baxter, and of George Fox, founder of the Quakers:

Richard Baxter (1615–91).
Nonconformist spokesman in the 1660s.

*Gildas Salvianus;*

THE

**REFORMED**
PASTOR.

Shewing the nature of the Paftoral work; Efpecially in Private Inftruction and Catechizing.

With an open CONFESSION of our too open SINS.

Prepared for a day of Humiliation kept at *Worcefter, Decemb.* 4 1655. by the Minifters of that County, who fubfcribed the Agreement for Catechizing and Perfonal Inftruction, at their entrance upon that work.

By their unworthy fellow-fervant
*Richard Baxter.*

Teacher of the Church at *Kederminfter.*

The fecond Edition, with an Appendix, in anfwer to fome Objections.

Luke 12. 47. [E' κεῖνος ἢ ὁ δῦλΘ ὁ γνὺς τὸ θέλημα τᾶ κυρίεέχυτᾶ, ὰ μὴ ἐτοιμάσας, μηδὲ πσιήσας αρὸς τὸ θέλημα αὐτᾶ, δαρήσε-) πολλός.]

*London,* Printed by *Robert White,* for *Nevil Simmons,* Book-feller at *Kederminfter,* and are to be fold by *Jofeph Nevill,* at the Plough in *Pauls* Church-Yard. 1657.

- Baxter, Richard. *Reliquiae Baxterianae . . . .* (1696).
- Keeble, N.H., & Nuttall, Geoffrey F., ed. *Calendar of the correspondence of Richard Baxter.* (2 vols. Clarendon Press, 1991).

A new edition of Baxter's *Reliquiae* is in preparation; for details, visit:

- A Scholarly Edition of Richard Baxter's Reliquiae Baxterianae (1696)
  **http://gtr.rcuk.ac.uk/projects?ref=AH/I000461/1**

For George Fox's writings, see:

- Fox, George. *The Journal of George Fox,* ed. John L. Nickalls. (Religious Society of Friends, 1997. Originally published Cambridge, 1952).

- Fox, George. *George Fox: an autobiography*, ed. Rufus Matthew Jones. (Ferris & Leach, 1909). Available online at **www.strecorsoc.org/gfox/title.html**

John Bunyan is perhaps the best-known Baptist Nonconformist of the seventeenth century, on account of his authorship of *Pilgrim's Progress*. His autobiography, *Grace Abounding to the Chief of Sinners*, tells us how he fell foul of the Cavalier Parliament's penal legislation. His record of his dialogues with Justices, the Bedfordshire Clerk of the Peace and the Assize judges, demonstrate their varying attitudes towards Dissent.[11]

Philip Doddridge was an important figure amongst Independents in the early eighteenth century. Like Baxter, he corresponded widely; his letters are edited in:

- Nuttall, Geoffrey F., ed. *Calendar of the correspondence of Philip Doddridge (1702-1751)*. (Northamptonshire Record Society 29, 1979. Also published as Historical Manuscripts joint publication 26, HMSO, 1979). See also Nuttall's *Philip Doddridge: additional letters. A supplement to Calendar of the correspondence of Philip Doddridge (1977)*. (Dr. Williams Trust, 2001).

The Wesley brothers had a huge influence in the late eighteenth century; John Wesley in particular travelled the length and breadth of the country. His works, which include not only letters, but also sermons, hymns, journals, etc., contain much information of local interest. There are various different editions and collections of extracts, but the latest is:

- Wesley, John. *The Works of John Wesley*, ed. Albert C. Outler. (26 vols; in progress. Clarendon Press, 1984– . Vols 1–4: Sermons. Vol. 7: A collection of hymns for the use of the people called Methodists Vol. 8 [Unpublished] Vol. 9: The Methodist societies. Vol. 10: The Methodist societies: the minutes of conference. Vol. 11: The appeals to men of reason and religion and certain related open letters. Vols 12–14: Doctrinal and controversial treatises. Vols 18–24: Journals and Diaries. Vols. 25–6: Letters 1721–53.)

Charles Wesley's journal is edited in:

• Kimbrough, S.T., & Newport, Kenneth G.C., eds. *The Manuscript Journal of the Reverend Charles Wesley, M.A.* (2 vols. Abingdon Press, 2007).

For a guide to his other manuscripts, see:

• Lloyd, Gareth. 'Charles Wesley's manuscripts: a guide to provenance and location', *Bulletin of the John Rylands University Library of Manchester* 88(2), 2006, pp.121–31.

Many of the works of both Charles and John Wesley are digitized at:

• The Wesley Center Online
 **http://wesley.nnu.edu**

The activities of all of these men were nationwide in their scope and their works include much valuable information about Nonconformity in particular places.

Many other Nonconformist autobiographies, collections of letters, sermons, tracts and other works are also available. Large collections are held by Dr. Williams's Library, by the John Rylands University Library of Manchester, by Harris Manchester College, Oxford and by most of the other specialist libraries listed below. Others can be found by consulting online union catalogues. Many papers of prominent Nonconformists are listed in:

• Royal Commission on Historical Manuscripts. *Papers of British churchmen, 1780-1940.* (HMSO, 1987).

Printed and manuscript diaries are listed by:

• Matthews, W. *British Diaries: an annotated bibliography of British diaries written between 1442 and 1942.* (University of California Press, 1950).

This bibliography is complemented by:

- Batts, J.S. *British Manuscript Diaries of the Nineteenth Century: an Annotated Listing*. (Centaur Press, 1976).
- Havlice, P.P. *And So to Bed; a Bibliography of Diaries Published in English*. (Scarecrow Press, 1987).

See also:

- Huff, Cynthia. *British Women's Diaries: a Descriptive Bibliography of Selected Nineteenth-Century Women's Manuscript Diaries*. (AMS Press, 1985).

Sermons and religious tracts may also be useful. Many were published in the nineteenth century and earlier; large collections are held in many libraries and record offices. Tracts were frequently used by evangelicals to discourage 'evil practises' amongst the lower orders. They frequently provide evidence of bigotry and prejudice, but they also offer an authentic picture of how the lower classes were viewed by their 'betters'. They also offer evidence of working-class behaviour and may provide surprisingly localized information. The predominant content of sermons is, of course, the theology of their times; and they may sometimes be dry reading. But they do provide valuable evidence of social mores. Funeral sermons may sometimes provide useful biographical information. For a discussion of religious tracts, see:

- Trinder, Barrie. 'Religious tracts as sources of local history: some West Midlands examples', *Local Historian* 10, 1972–3, pp.116–24.

Many important Nonconformist writings are included in:

- Sell, Alan P.F., ed. *Protestant Nonconformist texts*. 4 vols. Ashgate, 2006–7. Vol. 1. *1550-1700*, ed. R. Tudur Jones, et al. Vol. 2. *The Eighteenth Century*, ed. Alan P.F. Sell, et al. Vol. 3. *The Nineteenth Century*, ed. D.W. Bebbington et al. Vol. 4. *The Twentieth Century*, ed. David M. Thompson, et al.

There are two useful collections of nineteenth-century writings:

- Briggs, J.H.Y., & Sellers, I., eds. *Victorian Nonconformity.* Documents of modern history. (Edward Arnold, 1973).
- Thompson, David M., ed. *Nonconformity in the Nineteenth Century.* (Routledge & Kegan Paul, 1972).

## CONTEMPORARY NONCONFORMIST PERIODICALS

For the nineteenth century, the periodical press is perhaps the most important source of information for Nonconformist history. Altholz (see p.56 below) suggests that perhaps 3,000 different religious periodicals circulated in Britain between 1760 and 1900. All the major denominations had their own yearbooks, which generally list churches and ministers, and allow their histories to be traced. They also had their own journals, which often included obituaries, as well as more general denominational news. In the early nineteenth century, journals published by missionary organizations predominated. Thereafter, the number of journals published by temperance organizations increased dramatically. There were also a number of Nonconformist journals and newspapers of wider appeal. The *Evangelical Magazine* (monthly; 1793–1904), for example, had much local news. Weeklies, such as the *Patriot* (1832–66) and the *Nonconformist* (1841–80) and dailies edited by Dissenters, such as the *Manchester Guardian* and the *Leeds Mercury*, provide much information on the political and religious activities of Nonconformity. The Nonconformist *British Weekly* was responsible for the valuable 1888 survey of church attendance in London which has already been mentioned.

Many of these magazines can be downloaded from the websites listed above, p.27 and similar sites. Some Nonconformist periodicals are held in virtually all the libraries mentioned in this book. Most, however, are held by the British Library. For a guide to its collection, visit:

- British Library Collection Guides: Newspapers
  **www.bl.uk/collection-guides/newspapers**

More information about periodicals is given in the denominational chapters below, which also identify a number of indexes to obituaries in journals. For a detailed listing of religious periodicals in Britain, 1760–1900, see:

• Altholz, Josef L. *The Religious Press in Britain, 1760-1900.* (Greenwood, 1989).

For periodicals in theological libraries, consult:

• ABTAPL: Union list of Periodicals and other resources held by British theological and philosophical libraries **https://abtapl.wordpress.com/?uol_r=f3695493**

### THE STUDY OF CHAPEL BUILDINGS AND THEIR CONTENTS

Most Nonconformist church buildings were known as 'chapels'. The term 'church' was reserved for the people rather than the building. This usage distinguishes them from Anglicans and Roman Catholics, who use the term 'chapel' for a variety of different buildings and legal entities.

Few Nonconformist chapels were built prior to 1688. Many were built by the old Dissent in the eighteenth century and by the Methodists in the nineteenth century. Dissenting causes frequently began by meeting in houses, barns, or anywhere else they could find a meeting room. Some took many years to acquire their own chapel. Most chapels can be identified by using nineteenth-century trade directories such as those issued by Kelly's. These directories are listed, with locations, in:

• Norton, Jane E. *Guide to the national and provincial directories of England and Wales, excluding London, published before 1856.* (Royal Historical guides and handbooks 5, 1950).
• Shaw, Gareth, & Tipper, Alison. *British directories: a bibliography and guide to directories published in England and Wales (1850-1950) and Scotland (1773-1950).* (2nd ed. Mansell Publishing, 1997).

Many directories are available online at:

• Historical Directories
  **http://specialcollections.le.ac.uk/cdm/landingpage/
  collection/p16445coll4**

   Chapel buildings themselves can be made to yield much information about their history. Useful guidance on recording their architectural and archaeological details is provided by:

• *Hallelujah! Recording chapels and meeting houses.* (Council for
  British Archaeology, 1985).

Despite the fact that it is more concerned with Anglican buildings, it is also worth consulting:

• Parsons, David. *Churches and Chapels: Investigating Places of
  Worship.* Practical handbooks in archaeology 8. (2nd ed. Council
  for British Archaeology, 1989).

The architecture of Nonconformist chapels is the prime interest of:

• The Chapels Society
  **www.chapelssociety.org.uk**
  The Society publishes a newsletter which has many useful articles.

Many redundant Nonconformist chapels are cared for by:

• Historic Chapels Trust
  **www.hct.org.uk**
  The website includes historical notes on chapels in its care.

A number of works on the chapels of specific denominations are mentioned in denominational chapters below. General works include:

- Cherry, Bridget, ed. *Dissent & the Gothic Revival*. (Chapel Society, 2007).
- Lindley, Kenneth Arthur. *Chapels and Meeting Houses*. (John Baker, 1969).

Christopher Stell has compiled a number of detailed architectural surveys of chapels in the regions:

- Stell, Christopher. *Nonconformist Chapels and Meeting Houses in Central England*. (Royal Commission on the Historical Monuments of England, 1986).
- Stell, Christopher. *Nonconformist Chapels and Meeting Houses in Eastern England*. (English Heritage, 2001).
- Stell, Christopher. *Nonconformist Chapels and Meeting Houses in the North of England*. (Royal Commission on the Historical Monuments of England, 1994).
- Stell, Christopher. *Nonconformist Chapels and Meeting Houses in South-West England*. (Royal Commission on the Historical Monuments of England, 1991).

For Welsh chapels, see:

- Jones, Anthony. *Welsh Chapels*. (2nd ed. 1996).
- Capel: Cymdeithas Treftadaeth Capeli: The Chapels Heritage Society
  **www.capeli.org.uk**

A bibliography of Welsh chapel history is provided by:

- Independent Chapels of Wales
  **www.llgc.org.uk/information-for/researchers/bibliography/ independent-chapels-of-wales/**

The internal arrangements of chapels, specifically their seating, has been studied in:

• Skidmore, Chris, ed. *Sitting in Chapel*. (Chapels Society Journal 1, 2013).

## NONCONFORMIST PLATE

Every chapel where communion services are conducted needs suitable utensils. Many have had vessels specially made, sometimes with memorial inscriptions. For a recent survey, which records many inscriptions naming individuals, see:

• Stell, Christopher. *Nonconformist Communion Plate & Other Vessels*. Occasional publication 4. (The Chapels Society, 2008).

## NONCONFORMIST REGISTERS

Nonconformist registers are essential sources for family historians, and a mine of information for local historians. They provide the basis for understanding the sociological structure of Nonconformist congregations. Used with sources such as other church records, the census, trade directories and poll books/electoral registers, they enable us to determine the social status of Nonconformists and may even be used to discover their political loyalties.

The attitude of governments towards Nonconformists changed dramatically between the seventeenth and the nineteenth centuries. At the Restoration, they were viewed with great suspicion and subjected to strict controls. In the nineteenth century, those controls were either abolished, or put to uses that the Nonconformists themselves desired. The Worship Register, for example, provides a variety of benefits for those who register. And many Nonconformist registers of births/baptisms, marriages and deaths/burials survive today because the government decided to take them into its care in the mid-nineteenth century.

Nonconformist registers are known from as early as 1644, although survivals from the years of the Civil War and Interregnum are rare. The legislation of 1653, which instituted the keeping of civil registers of births, marriages and deaths, made the keeping of church registers superfluous. The only denomination which had organized a system of registration prior to the Restoration were the Quakers, following a request George Fox made in 1656.

After 1662, some of the ejected clergy began to keep registers. In some cases, it would be more correct to say that they continued to keep registers. The register of the Independent chapel at Northowram,[12] for example, was begun by Oliver Heywood when he was curate of Coley Chapelry (Yorkshire) and continued after he

*Oliver Heywood (1629–1702), compiler of the Northowram register.*

# THE

# Nonconformist Register,

## Of Baptisms, Marriages, and Deaths,

Compiled by the

## REVS OLIVER HEYWOOD & T. DICKENSON,

### 1644-1702,  1702-1752,

Generally known as the

# Northowram or Coley Register,

But comprehending numerous notices of Puritans and Anti-
Puritans in Yorkshire, Lancashire, Cheshire,
London, &c.

## With Lists of Popish Recusants, Quakers, &c.

———•◦•———

## EDITED BY J. HORSFALL TURNER.

———•◦•———

## FIVE ILLUSTRATIONS.

———•◦•———

BRIGHOUSE:
J. S. JOWETT, PRINTER, "NEWS" OFFICE.

MDCCCLXXXI.

*The Northowram Register.*

was ejected. Such registers were frequently regarded as the personal property of the minister. They were not congregational property, but could be used by ministers to record vital events in all the churches where they served as a pastor. Such registers included events from wide areas. Indeed, even those registers which were confined to particular congregations might still record events concerning people who lived some miles from the chapel. Nonconformist congregations often drew their members from a much wider area than a single parish.

For some churches, persecution forbade the keeping of registers. Maintaining documentary evidence of church membership was not wise in times of repression. Such evidence could be used against you. It was not until after that threat was lifted that the keeping of registers became widespread. Even then, only a few registers (apart from the Quakers) recorded marriages, and burials were frequently only recorded where Nonconformists had their own burial grounds. Most Nonconformist register entries were for baptisms and/or births. Baptists, of course, did not baptize babies, so their registers of baptisms are of adults – although they may have kept registers of births as well. Quakers did not baptize at all, but did record births. Sometimes Nonconformist entries were duplicated in parish registers. This applied particularly during the periods when a tax was imposed on baptisms.

The majority of Nonconformist marriages and burials were recorded in Anglican parish registers. The refusal of some Church of England clergymen to marry those who had not been baptised meant that Baptists – who might marry before baptism – registered marriages more frequently than other denominations.

From 1753 until 1837, it was illegal for anyone to marry outside of the Church of England, unless they were Jews or Quakers. Therefore, Nonconformist marriage registers (other than those of the Quakers) were not kept during this period. After the introduction of civil registration in 1837, marriages could be held in Non-conformist chapels, but only in the presence of a registrar, who entered the details into the civil registers. It was not until 1898 that Nonconformist churches were given the right to appoint an 'authorized person' to register marriages and report them to the Registrar General. Registers listing 'authorized persons' are now in The National Archives, class RG 42 (up until 1931). Since 1898, Nonconformist marriage registers have been almost identical to those of the Church of England (see below, p.66). Registers which are not still in use may sometimes be found deposited in county record offices.

Few Nonconformist congregations, apart from the Quakers, had their own burial grounds. In the century after the Restoration, most Dissenters were buried in the parish churchyard. In the nineteenth century, they were frequently buried in the new municipal cemeteries, which frequently had separate areas set aside for particular denominations. Cemetery registers frequently indicate denominations.

In London, Bunhill Fields was an important Nonconformist cemetery and was extensively used between the seventeenth to the nineteenth centuries. Perhaps 120,000 bodies are buried there. Its registers from 1713 are in The National Archives, classes RG 4 and RG 8. 47,682 index entries from these registers, 1788 to 1853, are included in the pay per view:

• National Burial Index for England and Wales
  **http://search.findmypast.com/search-world-records/**
  **national-burial-index-for-england-and-wales**

In addition, London Metropolitan Archives holds interment order books and transcripts of Bunhill Fields inscriptions, 1789–1854. See also:

• Crippens, G. 'The Tombs in Bunhill Fields', *Transactions of the Congregational Historical Society* 4, 1909–10, pp.347–63.

The quality of the registers kept by Nonconformists varies considerably. The Quakers were very careful with theirs, making considerable efforts to ensure accuracy. Others could be equally assiduous – or could neglect the duty altogether. Sometimes registers were kept in books that were also used for minutes, lists of members, or liturgical purposes. Others were kept on loose sheets of paper, perhaps subsequently being written up in more permanent form.

Entries could be very brief, but they could also be quite extensive. Dates of birth, as well as dates of baptism, are more frequently given than in parish registers, as are mothers' maiden names. Private baptisms are frequently recorded. Adult baptisms were, of course, the norm in Baptist circles, but other denominations also recorded them. Quakers who were disgruntled with the rigid control of their personal life exercised by their Meetings needed to be baptised when they changed their religious affiliations.

Dating methods used in the registers of most denominations conform to the pattern usually used in parish registers. The principal exception to this rule, again, are the Quakers, who followed their own usage for the names of days and months (see below, p.144). Many Nonconformists did, however, anticipate the switch from the Gregorian to the Julian calendar and began to use the new style of dating (which began the year on 1 January rather than 25 March) before Parliament decided to authorize the Crown to do so in 1752.

The Stamp Duty Act of 1785 imposed a tax on baptisms. This duty was collected assiduously by Nonconformists, as it was thought (erroneously) to confer legal validity on their registers. Subsequently, the courts held that Nonconformist registers had no such validity, but many do record the payment of duty between 1785 and the abolition of the tax in 1794. Indeed, in some places, registers were started in order to record the duty payable.

Registers were important to Nonconformists. The fact that they had no legal validity prior to 1837 was of great concern. Certificates of baptism in particular were used for the same purposes in the eighteenth century as the General Register Office's birth certificates are used now. Appointments to posts in the civil service and the armed forces required baptismal certificates, but those issued by Nonconformist ministers were frequently not acceptable. One of the prime political aims of Nonconformist campaigners was to persuade Parliament to validate their registers. That aim was achieved in 1837, with the passing of legislation to create a new system of civil registration.

The introduction of civil registration caused the government to review its attitude towards Nonconformist and other non-parochial registers and to conduct an inquiry into their status. Nonconformists had been lobbying the government for many years, demanding that their registers should have equal status with Anglican parish registers. The Commissioners appointed agreed, but recommended that Nonconformist registers should first be deposited with the Registrar General and 'authenticated'. In 1841, all non-Anglican churches were requested to deposit their records. Their response varied from enthusiasm to refusal. Roman Catholics mostly refused. The Quakers had their registers copied into 'digests' before they were deposited. Other churches showed greater enthusiasm. A number which had not previously kept registers hastened to compile them so that they could be deposited. The registers collected by the Commissioners are now in The National Archives, class RG 4 and have been digitized (see below).

These registers were closely inspected for the authenticity of their entries. Registers which were not regarded as authentic were returned to the churches which had sent them in. Such registers may still be with other church records – or they may have been lost. Their evidence may have been rejected by the Commissioners, but they could still be useful to the historian. A further collection of registers was made in 1857. The registers then deposited are now in The National Archives, class RG 8 and have also been digitized.

One reason for reluctance to deposit registers was that they were sometimes written in books which had also been used for other church memoranda, such as minutes of meetings and membership rolls. Examples of such books can be found amongst the deposited registers. Sometimes, pages of memoranda other than registers were torn out of such books and can now be found with church archives.

Since 1837, most Nonconformist churches have not kept birth/baptism and death/burial registers. There are two exceptions to this rule. Baptismal registers are maintained by those churches whose rules link baptism to membership. Since the Registration of

Burials Act of 1864, those churches which maintain burial grounds have been required by law to keep burial registers.

Civil registration procedures did make provision for registering Nonconformist marriage, although until 1898 there were no separate registers. District registrars had to be present in order to register ceremonies. After 1898, that ceased to be the case. From then on, congregations were empowered to appoint their own 'authorized persons', who kept their own registers. These were (and are) kept in duplicate, in books supplied by the Registrar General. One copy is retained by the church (and may sometimes be found deposited in local record offices), the other is returned to the district registrar on completion. The authorized person is required to make quarterly returns to the Registrar General, who may be asked to supply registration certificates for specific marriages. These can also be supplied by district registrars.

The pre-printed registers used by Nonconformists are almost identical to those used by the Church of England. The only differences are the absence of reference to 'the rites and ceremonies of the established church' ('established' is replaced by a blank space for completion), 'in the parish of' becomes 'in the district of' and the form is to be signed by the authorized person. The minister may be the authorized person, but if he is not, he can, if he wishes, sign above the signature of that individual.

Nonconformist registers are essential sources for family historians. They can also be invaluable to the local historian. Used with sources such as poll books, trade directories and other church records, they provide the basic information needed to reconstruct the social structure of Nonconformist churches and communities. Further information is given in two articles:

- Ambler, Rodney William. 'Non-parochial registers and the local historian', *Local Historian* 10(2), 1972, pp.59–64.
- Welch, Charles Edwin. 'Nonconformist registers', *Journal of the Society of Archivists* 2(9), 1964, pp.411–17.

### National Registration by Nonconformists
The registers deposited in 1841 included two attempts at national registration of Nonconformists. The Wesleyan Metropolitan Registry

is discussed below, p.163. The Protestant Dissenters Registry was established to register the births of Dissenters (although it could be used by anyone). It was maintained at Dr. Williams's Library, although it is now in The National Archives, class RG 5, and entries are available online. The Registry was established in 1742, although it includes retrospective entries dating back to 1716. Births were registered rather than baptisms, in deference to the Baptists. Nevertheless, a handful of baptisms were registered. After 1768, a separate book was used to register them. In order to register a child's birth, parents had to produce a certificate in duplicate, signed by their minister, the midwife and others present at the birth. This gave the name and sex of the child, the names of its parents, the maternal grandfather's name and the date and place of birth. These particulars were entered in the register, one of the certificates was filed and the other returned to the parents with a certificate of registration. After 1828, the procedure was varied. The certificate had to include the signatures of the parents. The register became merely a calendar to the certificates, which became the main record. Entries ceased in 1837, when the register was deposited with the Registrar General. There are almost 49,000 entries.

Another attempt to create a national register had been made in 1747, at the College of Arms. It was unsuccessful, although a handful of events were recorded.

### Locating Nonconformist Registers

All the registers in RG 4, RG 5, RG 6 (the Quaker registers – see pp.134–7) and RG 8 have been digitized and are available on the internet. A detailed guide (which you should read before searching) is available with the pay per view database at:

- BMD Registers
  **www.bmdregisters.co.uk**

A printed catalogue of the registers in both RG 4 and RG 8 is also available:

- *General Register Office: Registers of births, marriages and deaths, surrendered to the non-parochial registers commissions, RG4 and RG8.* (2 vols. List and Index Society 265–6, 1996). This supersedes the Society's vol. 42 and older lists. It does not cover Quaker registers. For these, see below, pp.134–7.

Most of these registers are also indexed in the *International Genealogical Index* (*IGI*), at Family Search **http://familysearch.org** (which is free). A fiche version of the *IGI* is widely available in libraries. A CD version, known as the *British Vital Records Index*, is also available. If you find an entry in the *IGI*, you should consult the original register, as it may well contain much more information than the bare index entry can provide. Microfilm of all registers indexed by the *IGI* can be obtained through the Family History Centres of the Church of Jesus Christ of Latter Day Saints.

Not all pre-1837 Nonconformist registers were deposited with the Registrar General. Many were retained by congregations, but have since been deposited in record . offices and denominational repositories. Some can be identified through internet union catalogues (listed above, pp.28–9). Surviving registers are listed in detail in the county volumes of the *National Index of Parish Registers*. Welsh registers are listed in:

- Ifans, Dafydd. *Cofrestri anghydffurfiol Cymru = Nonconformist registers of Wales.* (National Library of Wales / Welsh Archivists Group, 1994.)

Registers for specific denominations are listed in the relevant guides in the Society of Genealogists' *My ancestors were . . .* series. Full details are given in the denominational chapters below. It is also worth checking record office websites for lists of the registers they hold.

A handful of Nonconformist registers have been published. These are listed in the county volumes of Raymond's *British Genealogical Library Guides* (formerly *British Genealogical Bibliographies*). Family history societies have been responsible for some of these publications. Details are usually given on the 'publications' pages of their websites, which are listed at:

• Genuki: Family History and Genealogy Societies
  **www.genuki.org.uk/Societies**

## OTHER LOCAL CHURCH RECORDS

The term 'Nonconformist records' should not be treated as synonymous with 'Nonconformist registers'. A wide variety of other records are available: minutes, accounts, lists of members, trust deeds, church magazines and a variety of other documents. The records of Sunday Schools (see below), womens' meetings and other church organizations may also be found. These sources contain valuable information and are essential documents for local historians. They often contain illuminating information on matters as diverse as membership, finance, the pastorate, furnishings, buildings, discipline and church activities. Family historians should not ignore these records, as they may offer much interesting information about ancestors' activities. Some families were associated with particular churches for generations, if not centuries, and chapel records may be very informative about them – although the distinction between church members and adherents should be borne in mind. Church members were the committed, who participated in the decision-making process. Adherents, who were frequently more numerous than members, took little part in decision-making, but attended church services and activities and thronged chapel and Sunday School anniversaries. They are less likely to be well documented.

Many congregations have deposited their records in local record offices. Others have deposited them in some of the specialist repositories mentioned elsewhere in this book. Local record office websites frequently list their holdings. For London, see:

• London Metropolitan Archives: Records of Nonconformists in London
  **www.cityoflondon.gov.uk/things-to-do/london-metropolitan -archives/visitor-information/Documents/03- Nonconformist-records-at-lma.pdf**

Most records formerly at the Guildhall Library have been transferred to London Metropolitan Archives. The Guildhall Library guides, however, are still useful:

- Guildhall Library Manuscripts Section General Guide 17: Non Anglican Religious Bodies
  **www.history.ac.uk/gh/17.htm**
- *Nonconformist, Roman Catholic, Jewish and Burial Ground Registers.* (3rd ed. Guildhall Library Publications, 2002).

Many London Nonconformist records can also be found in Dr. Williams's Library (see above, pp.31–2).

## SUNDAY SCHOOLS
In the eighteenth and nineteenth centuries, many churches established Sunday Schools for children who could not attend during the week, as they were working. These were intended to draw children into churches, as well as to provide instruction in reading and writing. In 1885, an astonishing 19 per cent of the eligible population were enrolled.[13] The extent to which they were successful locally is a matter for the local historian. The registers they kept may prove useful to the family historian. Records may be found with the records of individual churches. There were also a number of national Sunday School organizations. For discussions of the Sunday School movement, see:

- Cliff, Philip B. *The Rise and Development of the Sunday School Movement in England, 1780-1980.* (National Christian Education Council, 1986).
- Orchard, Stephen, & Briggs, J.H.Y., eds. *The Sunday School Movement: studies in the growth and decline of Sunday Schools.* (Paternoster, 2007).

Welsh Sunday Schools are listed in:

- *Report of the Commissioners of Inquiry into the State of Education in Wales.* HC 870 (1847), XXIII. (1); HC871 (1847) XXVII. (2); HC872 (1847), XXVII (2), 339.

## SCHOOLS

Nineteenth-century Nonconformists also interested themselves in day schools. A full survey of Nonconformist schools was made in 1861 for the Royal Commission on Popular Education and published as a Parliamentary paper. See:

- *Report to the Commission . . . by the Committee appointed by them for the purpose of obtaining an enumeration of Dissenters schools.* Parliamentary paper 1861, XXXXVIII.

Many schools were operated by the Nonconformist British and Foreign School Society. A list of 'British Schools' for 1897 is available online. Its annual reports also include lists of schools connected with the Society and details of subscribers. The report for 1877 also includes a list of all students trained at the Society's teacher training colleges since 1810. The Society's archives enable teachers to be traced from their original applications to enter its colleges, through their student years, and through their various appointments in Society schools until eventual retirement. They also provide much information for local historians about the schools the Society supported. See:

- British and Foreign School Society: Archive
  **www.bfss.org.uk/archive**
- Brunel University: British and Foreign School Society (BFSS) Collection
  **www.brunel.ac.uk/services/archives-management/ university-collections/british-and-foreign-school-society- collection**
- Bartle, George F. 'The Records of the British and Foreign School Society', *Genealogists Magazine* 23(3), 1989, pp.102–3.

## MONUMENTAL INSCRIPTIONS

Most Nonconformists placed memorials to the deceased in their chapels and burial grounds. Even the Quakers, who originally condemned the practice as 'vain', began to raise stones in the mid-nineteenth century. Members of the same family were often buried close together. Their inscriptions may help to sort out tangled webs of family relationships. Many inscriptions have been transcribed and copies of the transcripts deposited in local studies libraries, family history societies and the Society of Genealogists.

Some Nonconformist burial grounds have been closed and their stones removed. Records of such removals, including plans of burial grounds and details of inscriptions, have been kept since 1911. They are in The National Archives class RG 37. Records of exhumations and re-interments between 1887 and 1901 are also held in The National Archives, class HO 85.

## CEMETERIES
Reference has already been made to cemetery registers. The difficulties faced by Nonconformists in burying their dead meant that they frequently led the way in the establishment of cemetery companies in the nineteenth century. A study of the history of cemeteries in a particular area may reveal a great deal about the politics of religion and opposition to the established church's near- monopoly of graveyards. A variety of sources are available for this study. There are various reports amongst the Parliamentary papers and from Chadwick's Board of Health. The records of cemetery companies provide useful information, as do newspaper reports and town guides. A useful introduction to this material is provided by:

• Rugg, Julie. 'Researching early nineteenth-century cemeteries: sources and methods', *Local Historian* 28(3), 1998, pp.130–44.

## MISSIONARY RECORDS
Since the eighteenth century, and in some cases earlier, Nonconformists have engaged in overseas mission. The work has depended upon local congregations being prepared to raise money and to recruit missionaries. Local auxiliaries were established to support overseas work. Children collected their farthings, women met in sewing circles to raise money and churches were occasionally enthralled by

missionaries home on leave recounting their experiences. Support for overseas mission frequently invigorated local churches. Engagement in overseas mission is therefore an important aspect of their history.

The record of support for missionary endeavours is extensive and could be the focus of interesting research by both local and family historians. To what extent did local churches provide support? Did they send out missionaries themselves? Did they keep in contact with missionaries? What was the nature of their support? Family historians with missionary ancestors are likely to discover much information about them in the archives, including numerous letters and photographs.

Over 400 collections of missionary archives are listed at:

• Mundus: Gateway to Missionary Collections in the UK
  **www.mundus.ac.uk**

A major collection of missionary archives is held by the School of Oriental and African Studies (SOAS) of the University of London:

• SOAS Library: Missionary Collections
  **www.soas.ac.uk/library/archives/collections/missionary-collections**

See the SOAS guide to:

• Tracing Your Missionary Ancestors
  **www.soas.ac.uk/library/archives/specialist-guides/subject/file76134.pdf**

A general history of missionary endeavour is provided by:

• Cox, Jeffrey. *The British Missionary Enterprise since 1700.*
  (Routledge, 2008).

**FURTHER READING**
A number of general guides to sources for the history of

Nonconformity are available, but none take into account the huge amount of information that is now available on the internet. Nevertheless, the archives which underlie internet-based information have not changed, and the following titles are still worth consultation:

- Gandy, Michael. *Tracing Nonconformist Ancestors*. (Public Record Office, 2001). Brief.
- Mullett, Michael. *Sources for the History of English Nonconformity, 1660-1830*. Archives and the user 8. (British Records Association, 1991). A scholarly review, outlining possibilities for research.
- Shorney, David. *Protestant Nonconformity and Roman Catholicism: a guide to sources in the Public Record Office*. (PRO Publications, 1996). Basic and only concerned with records in what is now The National Archives.
- Steel, D.J. *Sources for Nonconformist Genealogy and Family History*. National index of parish registers 2. (Society of Genealogists, 1973). The most comprehensive treatment for family historians, with excellent bibliographies of older publications.

For Nonconformity before 1660, see:

- Cross, Claire. 'Popular piety and the records of the unestablished churches. 1460-1660', in Baker, Derek, ed. *The materials, sources and methods of Ecclesiastical History*. Studies in Church History 11. (Ecclesiastical History Society, 1975), pp.269–92.

Regional guides are provided by:

- Building on History: Religion in London
  **www.open.ac.uk/Arts/religion-in-london/index.html**
  This includes resource guides on Baptists and Methodists, and on 'Black Majority Churches'. Its resource guide on 'religious censuses' includes a copy of the 1851 religious census for London, together with links to digitised censuses of 1886 and 1902–3 carried out by newspapers

- Garratt, Morris, ed. *Sure Coffers: some sources for the history of religion in the North West*. (Library Association Local Studies Group, 1987).
- Miscellanea Edintone: a collection of items on Nonconformity and Northamptonshire
  **www.edintone.com/Nonconformist_denominations**
- Ruston, Alan. *Nonconformity in Hertfordshire: a guide to sources for family and local historians*. Special publication 6. (Hertfordshire Family History Society, 2005).
- Ward, Graham. *Sources for researching Nonconformists in Northamptonshire*. (2nd ed. Northamptonshire Family History Society, 2011).

There are also a number of useful journal articles:

- Field, Clive D. 'Preserving Zion: the anatomy of Protestant Nonconformist archives in Great Britain and Ireland', *Archives* 33(11), 2008, pp.14–51.
- Morris, G.M. 'The Nonconformist chapel and the local community', *Local Historian* 10(5), 1973, pp.253–8.
- Powell, W.R., et al. 'Protestant Nonconformist records and the local historian', *Archives* 5, 1961, pp.1–12.
- Powell, W.R. 'The sources for the history of Protestant Nonconformist churches in England', *Bulletin of the Institute of Historical Research* 25, 1952, pp.213–27.

For a general discussion of the contrasting methodologies of sociologists and historians, see:

- Wilson, Bryan R. 'Methodological perspectives in the study of religious minorities', *Bulletin of the John Rylands University Library of Manchester* 70(3), 1988, pp.225–40.

**Wales**

For Wales, see:

• Roberts, Brynley Francis. 'Welsh Nonconformist archives',
  *Journal of Welsh Ecclesiastical History 3*, 1986, pp.61–72.

Much useful bibliographical information, including a list of denominational and historical journals, can be found at:

• Genuki Wales: Religion and Religious Life
  **www.genuki.org.uk/big/wal/Religion.html**

# Chapter 3

# THE THREE DENOMINATIONS

## A. GENERAL

The fluidity of relationships between Presbyterians, Independents and Baptists has already been stressed. There were, however, important differences. The Presbyterians did not want to leave the Church of England: their leaders were clergymen who had been expelled from the Church, rather than people who believed in the necessity of separation. They desired a reformed Church of England, rather than new denominations. Presbyterians sought to replace bishops with presbyteries, hoping to reclaim the Church of England rather than to develop separate structures.

Independents, by contrast, argued for separation and for the autonomy of each congregation. They became known as Congregationalists in the eighteenth century. Baptists too were separatists; their distinguishing mark was their rejection of infant baptism.

None of these three groups developed a strong denominational structure until the late eighteenth and nineteenth centuries, despite the emphasis the Presbyterians placed on the need for one, and despite the example of Presbyterians in Scotland (where they were the established church). In the 1690s, Presbyterians and Congregationalists (as the Independents came to be known) had come together in a 'Happy Union', but this fizzled out after a few years.

There were a few supra-denominational organizations. One of these was the Protestant Dissenting Deputies, founded in 1732. The Committee consisted of representatives from congregations within twelve miles of London. Their remit was to defend the civil rights of Dissenters. Although technically only representative of London congregations, in practice they were seen as representative of dissenting interests nationwide. Records are held by London Metropolitan Archives. For a history of their activities, see:

• Manning, Bernard Lord. *The Protestant Dissenting Deputies*, ed. Ormerod Greenwood. (Cambridge University Press, 1952).

There were also a few regional organizations which brought Presbyterians and Independents together. The minutes of a Lancashire assembly are held by Dr. Williams' Library. Those of the United Brethren of Devon and Cornwall have been published:

• Brockett, Allan, ed. *The Exeter Assembly: the minutes of the assemblies of the United Brethren of Devon and Cornwall, 1691-1717, as transcribed by the Reverend Isaac Gilling*. (Devon & Cornwall Record Society, New series 6, 1963).

Presbyterians and Congregationalists came together in 1972 to form the United Reformed Church. Its central archives since its foundation are held in the Congregational Library at Dr. Williams's Library. For details, visit:

• United Reformed Church Archive
  **www.urc.org.uk/urcarchive.html**

There are a number of non-governmental surveys of Nonconformist strength. The first derived from a previous attempt at unity. The Common Fund was set up in 1690 as a result of the 'Happy Union'. It aimed to support poor provincial ministers and congregations and began by undertaking a survey of Presbyterian and Congregational strength across the country. This survey has been published:

• Gordon, Alexander. *Freedom after Ejection: a review (1690-1692) of Presbyterian and Congregational Nonconformity in England and Wales*. (Manchester University Press, 1917).

Another survey is held in Dr. Williams's Library and indexed in:

• Creasey, John. *Index to the John Evans List of Dissenting Congregations and Ministers, 1715-1729, in Dr. Williams's Library.* (Dr. Williams Trust, 1964).

For the Bristol portion of this survey, see:

• Morgan, Kenneth, ed. 'The John Evans list of dissenting congregations and ministers in Bristol, 1715-1729', in Barry, Jonathan, & Morgan, Kenneth, eds. *Reformation and revival in eighteenth-Century Bristol.* (Bristol Record Society 45, 1994), pp.65–73.

Josiah Thompson's list of Dissenting congregations and many of their ministers is also held by Dr. Williams' Library and is printed in:

• 'A view of English Nonconformity in 1773', *Transactions of the Congregational Historical Society* 5, 1911–12, pp.205–22, 261–77 & 372–85.

See also:

• 'London conventicles in 1683', *Transactions of the Congregational Historical Society* 3, 1907–8, pp.364–6. This is supplemented by Whitley, W.T. 'Thompson list of conventicles in 1683', *Transactions of the Congregational Historical Society* 4, 1909–10, pp.49–53.

Josiah Thompson also compiled about 100 histories of particular congregations, which have not been published. His manuscripts are in Dr. Williams' Library.

### Dissenting Ministers
Some of the sources already mentioned provide much information on Dissenting ministers. Others held by Dr. Williams' Library focus

more specifically on them. The Walter Wilson manuscripts, compiled in the 1830s, are notes on Dissenting ministers and congregations throughout the country. The Surman Index was originally a card index of Dissenting ministers, but is now available online. It is not comprehensive, but includes many who attended theological colleges. The majority were Congregationalists, but there are some Presbyterians and some Baptists. See:

- The Surman Index Online
  **www.english.qmul.ac.uk/drwilliams/surman/intro.html**

A collection of nineteenth-century autobiographies is listed in:

- 'Ms autobiographies held by Dr. Williams's Library', *Transactions of the Congregational Historical Society* 16, 1945–51, pp.108–12.

A detailed biographical dictionary for the twentieth century is provided by:

- Binfield, Clyde, & Taylor, John, eds. *Who they were in the reformed churches of England and Wales, 1901-2000.* (United Reformed Church History Society, 2007).

Many obituaries of leading Nonconformists appeared in the *Gentleman's Magazine,*[1] and are indexed in:

- Ruston, Alan. *Obituaries and marriages of Dissenting ministers, in the Gentleman's Magazine in the 18th century.* (Alan Ruston, 1996).
- Ruston, Alan. *Obituaries and marriages of Dissenting ministers in the Gentleman's Magazine 1801-1837.* (Alan Ruston, 2008).

Other works of relevance are noted below under specific denominations. Researchers should also consult the innumerable biographies and autobiographies of Nonconformist ministers and laymen, which can be identified by searching library catalogues. They are likely to reveal much about church life that cannot be derived from formal congregational records.

## Dissenting Academies

The Dissenters were active educationalists. Much about them can be learnt from the records of their academies. Information concerning c.220 academies, c.700 tutors and c.11,000 students is provided by:

- Dissenting Academies Online
  **www.english.qmul.ac.uk/drwilliams/portal.html**

Many schoolmasters and their schools are listed in:

- 'Dissenters schools, 1660-1820', *Transactions of the Baptist Historical Society* 4(4), 1915, pp.220–7.

The histories of many Dissenting academies are outlined in:

- McLachland, H. *English Education under the Test Acts, being the History of the Nonconformist Academies, 1662-1821.* (Manchester University Press, 1931).

Tutors at Dissenting academies are listed by:

- A Biographical Dictionary of Tutors at the Dissenters' Private Academies, 1660–1729 (2013), by Mark Burden
  **www.qmulreligionandliterature.co.uk/online-publications/a-biographical-dictionary**
  This is also available as a printed book.

## B. THE PRESBYTERIANS AND UNITARIANS

The Presbyterians were the largest and most influential group of Dissenters in 1662. In practice, however, there was little to distinguish them from the Independents. Even in 1648, when they had been in the ascendant, they had failed to create a synodical structure on the Scottish model. After 1662, each congregation governed itself. They appointed their own ministers and church officers, they determined the form of their own worship, and they decided what registers and other records they needed to keep. The 'Happy Union' of 1690 had little impact on their governance.

Presbyterians tended to be of higher social standing than other Dissenters. They had considerable support amongst the gentry, who could mitigate the persecution to which they were subjected. But they found Dissent difficult. It involved exclusion from the public offices which their status would otherwise have given them. And they deplored the idea of separation. They expected an early accommodation with the Church of England. When that expectation receded from view, many rejoined the established church. Their theological differences were not felt to be sufficient to justify continued separation.

Theological turbulence within Dissenting congregations also had an impact on loyalties. Many Presbyterian churches became Unitarian in the mid-eighteenth century (although, for legal reasons, they frequently continued to call themselves Presbyterian). Presbyterians who held to Trinitarian beliefs frequently joined other denominations. Most Presbyterian congregations which remained orthodox became Congregationalists. They were sometimes influenced by the evangelical revival. By 1800 only a handful of Presbyterian churches continued to accept Trinitarian beliefs.

The emergence of Unitarianism was illegal. Anti-Trinitarianism was not legally tolerated, even by the Toleration Act of 1689. It was not until 1813 that congregations could legally use the Unitarian label and not until 1825 that the British and Foreign Unitarian Society was founded. Even then, the Unitarians frequently found themselves in legal difficulty, since the trust deeds of many of their chapels specified that they could only be used for Trinitarian worship. In the early nineteenth century, the Lady Hewley case provided a *cause célèbre* which helped influence Parliament to provide greater protection for Unitarian congregations. Lady Hewley's charity provided grants for a variety of Nonconformist causes, including the support of 'poor and godly preachers for the time being of Christ's holy gospel' belonging to all three dissenting denominations. However, by 1830 all its trustees were Unitarians. Their control was challenged in the courts in a long-running case, which was only settled in 1842 by a House of Lords ruling, which upheld the challengers and replaced the trustees. Many papers relating to the case are held by John Rylands University Library of Manchester. For a detailed account of the legal implications of Unitarianism, see:

- James, T.S. *The history of the litigation and legislation respecting Presbyterian chapels and charities in England and Ireland between 1816 and 1849.* (Hamilton Adams & Co., 1867). This book includes John Evans's list of Presbyterian and Independent chapels, 1717–29 and much further information.

The issue concerning Unitarian ownership of chapels was eventually resolved by the Dissenters' Chapels Act, 1844. This established the title of congregations who had used the same premises for the previous twenty-five years. See:

- Montgomery, R. Mortimer. 'The significance of the Dissenters' Chapels Act of 1844', *Transactions of the Unitarian Historical Society* 8(2), 1944, pp.45–51. See also pp.52–7.
- Long, Arthur. 'What did Mr Gladstone say in 1844? The Dissenters' Chapel Act after 150 years', *Transactions of the Unitarian Historical Society* 20, 1991–4, pp.233–70; 21, 1995–8, pp.43–55.

Unitarianism was not a popular creed. It made no evangelical proclamation and failed to participate in the growth of religious enthusiasm in the early nineteenth century. Unitarian congregations needed learned ministers to preach its sermons, but few were available.

Presbyterianism, however, underwent a resurgence in the early nineteenth century, encouraged by the missionary endeavours of Scottish Presbyterians. A number of new churches were founded on the Scottish model, with full synodical government and Trinitarian beliefs. They joined with the few remaining English Presbyterians to found the Presbyterian Church of England in 1836. In 1972, the denomination merged with Congregationalists and others to form the United Reformed Church.

Many of the leading figures of churches which disappeared in the eighteenth century are mentioned in Turner's *Original Records* (above, p.44). For Cheshire, reference may be made to:

• Gordon, Alexander, ed. *Cheshire classis minutes 1691-1745.* (Chiswick Press, 1919).

For a general survey of Presbyterian and Unitarian churches, which includes details of all churches in existence in 1897, including dates of foundations and lists of ministers, see:

• Evans, George Eyre. *Vestiges of protestant Dissent, being lists of ministers, sacramental plate, registers, antiquities and other matters pertaining to most of the churches (and a few others) included in the National Conference of Unitarian, Liberal Christian, Free Christian, Presbyterian and other non-subscribing or kindred congregations.* (1897).

### Central Records

The central records of the Presbyterian Church of England are held at Westminster College, Cambridge (not to be confused with the Methodist's Westminster College), which served as the denomination's theological college from 1844. The archives of Westminster College itself may also prove useful. See:

• Westminster College: Archives
  **www.westminster.cam.ac.uk/archives/collections-at-westminster.html**

The archives of the General Assembly of Unitarian and Free Churches and of various other Unitarian organizations, including the General Baptist Assembly, are held at Essex Hall. It also holds the records of many Unitarian congregations. For details, consult:

• Godfrey, Peter B., & Ditchfield, G. M. 'The Unitarian archives at Essex Hall', *Archives* 26(104), 2001, pp.58–70.

See also:

- Godfrey, Peter. 'Records held at Essex Hall', *Transactions of the Unitarian Historical Society* 22(1), 1999, pp.76–8.

Many Unitarian records are held by Dr. Williams's Library. These include, amongst others, the records of the British and Foreign Unitarian Association and of the General Assembly of Unitarian and Free Churches. There are also a few records of individual churches.

### Records of Individual Presbyterian and Unitarian Churches

Surviving records of Presbyterian and Unitarian churches, other than the registers, tend to focus on ministerial matters, buildings and finance. Presbyterian ministers had much greater authority than other Nonconformist ministers. Consequently, the appointment was much more important. There is much evidence on the procedures for choosing ministers and for involving other churches in that process, as well as for the conditions under which ministers were employed. By contrast, there is less information on disciplinary matters than in the records of most other denominations. Disciplinary oversight was exercised, if at all, by ministers, who kept no records. There are few censorious remarks on members in minute books. Minutes and accounts record administrative activities, such as building maintenance, charitable activities and the organization of church life. Registers of subscribers and records relating to pew rents provide valuable sociological information, as well as being interesting to family historians. Sunday Schools can be extensively documented and may include details of children attending and their parents. Seating plans and lists can be particularly informative. Who sat where, and how much they paid to do so, can be useful indicators of status. There is less information about Presbyterian poor. Presbyterians, unlike some other denominations, made no special provision for poor relief.

Most records of individual Presbyterian and Unitarian churches have been deposited in local record offices, or may still be with church secretaries. For a full listing of Unitarian congregations and their records, see:

• Unitarian Historical Society: location list of records
  **www.unitarianhistory.org.uk/hsrecords4.html**

See also:

• Hill, Andrew M. 'Unitarian congregations in Great Britain: a
  location list of their records', *Transactions of the Unitarian
  Historical Society* 17(3), 1981, pp.109–24; 17(4), 1982, pp.155–69;
  18(1), 1983, pp.46–50; 18(2), 1984, p.54; 18(3), 1985, p.164; 18(4),
  1986, p.236.

For published works on particular congregations, see:

• Bibliography of Unitarian Congregations which have Existed
  Since 1800 / Alan Ruston
  **www.unitarianhistory.org.uk/hsresearch4.html**
  Scroll down and click (five files).

Two regional studies provide useful accounts of particular
congregations and their ministers:

• Evans, George Eyre. *Record of the Provincial Assembly of
  Lancashire and Cheshire.* (Manchester: H. Rawson & Co., 1896).
  Lists the records and ministers of member churches.
• Murch, Jerom. *A history of the Presbyterian and General Baptist
  churches of the West of England, with memoirs of some of their
  pastors.* (R. Hunter, 1835).

### Presbyterian and Unitarian Registers

Registers of baptisms, marriages and burials predominate amongst
the records of individual Presbyterian and Unitarian congregations.
In the early days, such registers were frequently regarded as the
personal property of ministers, rather than as congregational records.
They had no set form, although printed registration books were
sometimes used. Registers frequently contain much more than
merely a bare record of names and dates. Many are now in The

National Archives and are available online (see above, pp.67–8). Registers are fully listed in Ruston's *My Ancestors were Presbyterians* (see below) and may also be identified in the county volumes of the Society of Genealogists' *National Index of Parish Registers* series.

### Presbyterian and Unitarian Chapels

An architectural gazetteer of Unitarian chapels (many of which were formerly Presbyterian) is provided in:

• Hague, Graham. *The Unitarian Heritage: an architectural survey of chapels and churches in the Unitarian tradition in the British Isles.* (P.B. Godfrey, 1986).

### Presbyterian and Unitarian Ministers

Obituaries of Unitarian ministers found in denominational journals have been indexed by Alan Ruston. See:

• Index to the Obituaries of Unitarian Ministers 1800–99 **www.unitarianhistory.org.uk/ministerobit18004.html** This is continued for 1900–2004 at **/ministerobit4.html**, with a supplementary list at **/pdfs/Supplement per cent202014 per cent20Proof per cent203X.pdf**

These webpages incorporate a number of printed indexes:

• Ruston, Alan. *Unitarian Obituaries, 1794-1850: index and synopsis.* (Alan Ruston, 1990).
• Ruston, Alan. *Obituaries of Unitarian ministers,1800-1849: index and synopsis.* Supplement to *Transactions of the Unitarian Historical Society* 24(1), 2007.
• Ruston, Alan. *Obituaries of Unitarian ministers, 1850-1899, index and synopsis.* Supplement to *Transactions of the Unitarian Historical Society* 23(3), 2005.
• Ruston, Alan. *Obituaries of Unitarian ministers, 1900-1999: index and synopsis. Transactions of the Unitarian Historical Society* 22(2), 2000, pp.163–246; supplement, 23(3), 2005.

- Ruston, Alan. *Monthly Repository, 1806-1832: index to and synopsis of the obituaries.* (Alan Ruston, 1985).

A Unitarian biographical dictionary is provided by:

- Carter, George. *Unitarian Biographical Dictionary: being short notices of the lives of noteworthy Unitarians and kindred thinkers brought down to the year 1900.* (Unitarian Christian Publishing Office, 1902).

For students who attended the Unitarian College, Manchester, see:

- McLachlan, H. *Unitarian College, Manchester, register of students 1854-1929.* (Manchester: c.1930).

Post-1794 obituaries from Unitarian and other journals, such as the *Monthly Repository* and the *Christian Reformer*, are indexed in:

- Unitarian Obituaries
  **www.unitarianobituaries.org.uk**

For Unitarian Members of Parliament, see:

- Bebbington, D.W. 'Unitarian Members of Parliament in the nineteenth century: a catalogue'. Supplement to *Transactions of the Unitarian Historical Society* 24(3), 2009. See also pp.153–75. This has been digitized at **www.unitarianhistory.org.uk/ hsresearch4.html**

There are also many biographies at:

- Dictionary of Unitarian and Universalist Biography
  **http://uudb.org**

**Presbyterian and Unitarian Periodicals and Yearbooks**
The wide range of Nonconformist journals in the nineteenth and

twentieth centuries are listed by Altholz (see above, p.56). The *English Presbyterian Messenger* (various titles, 1847–1966) was a leading Presbyterian journal. Unitarian titles included, amongst others, the *Monthly Repository* (1806–37) and the *Christian Reformer* (1815–63). The weekly *Inquirer* commenced in 1842. Unitarian yearbooks began with the *British and Irish Unitarian Almanack* (1847–51) and continued with the *Unitarian Almanac* (1852–64), the *Unitarian Pocket Book* (1864–90), the *Essex Hall Year Book* (1890–1928), the *General Assembly of Unitarian and Free Christian Churches (GA) Year Book* (1929– ) and the *Directory and Handbook* (1986– ). For the Presbyterians, consult *The Official Hand-book of the Presbyterian Church of England,* published from 1892 to 1971. Individual congregations and ministers can be traced through these yearbooks.

Presbyterians and Congregationalists had their own separate denominational historical societies prior to 1973, each publishing its own journal. The *Journal of the Presbyterian Historical Society of England* (1914–72) and the *Transactions of the Congregational History Society* (1901–72) were merged when the parent societies joined together in the:

• URC History Society
  **www.westminster.cam.ac.uk/rcl/about/urc-history-society**

This Society now publishes:

• *The Journal of the United Reformed Church History Society.* (1973–).

**Missionary Records**
Presbyterian Church of England Foreign Missions Committee records, 1842–1972, are held by SOAS. They include records relating to individual missionaries and are described at:

• Mundus: Presbyterian Church of England Foreign Missions
  Committee
  **www.mundus.ac.uk** (Search title)

**Presbyterian and Unitarian Record Offices.**
The collection of the Unitarian College, Manchester, is now deposited in the John Rylands University Library of Manchester. The College's own archives include various admission records, as well as a variety of minutes and records, 1854–1953. The collection also includes the archives of various other bodies, for example, minutes of the meetings of Presbyterian and Unitarian ministers in Lancashire and Cheshire, 1820–75 and minutes of the Monthly Conference of Ministers, 1882–1943. There are also many letters, diaries, texts of sermons and tracts, lecture notes, accounts and autobiographical material, c.1720–1943. For a full description, see:

• Field, Clive, & Shiel, Judith. 'The Unitarian College Collection and other Unitarian materials in the John Rylands University Library of Manchester', in Smith, Leonard, et al. *Unitarian to the Core: Unitarian College Manchester, 1854-2004*. (Carnegie Publishing, 2004), pp.177–84.

See also:

• University of Manchester Library: Unitarian College archives **www.library.manchester.ac.uk/search-resources/guide-to-special-collections/atoz/unitarian-college-archives**

The URC History Society collections, housed at Westminster College, Cambridge **www.westminster.cam.ac.uk/index.php/urc-history-society**, includes denominational yearbooks for all predecessor denominations (including Presbyterians, Congregationalists and Churches of Christ), denominational magazines such as the *Presbyterian Messenger* and the *Evangelical Magazine*, many church histories, a run of composite biographical files about Presbyterian ministers and various early printed books.

The Essex Hall Unitarian archives have already been mentioned (above, pp.84–5). Dr Williams Library (see above, pp.31–2) also has important Presbyterian and Unitarian collections.

**Guides to Sources**

A detailed guide to Presbyterian and Unitarian records, including a full list of registers, is provided by:

- Ruston, Alan. *My ancestors were English Presbyterians or Unitarians: how can I find out more about them?* (2nd ed. Society of Genealogists Enterprises, 2001).

See also:

- Hodson, J. Howard. 'The manuscript sources of Presbyterian history', *Transactions of the Unitarian Historical Society* 12(3), 1961, pp.98–110.
- Kelley, Lillian W. *Some Sources of English Presbyterian History*. (Presbyterian Historical Society of England, 1950). Reprinted from *Journal of the Presbyterian Historical Society of England* 9(3), 1950. Primarily of nineteenth-century interest.

For the records of individual congregations, see above, pp.85–6.

**Further Reading**
- Bolam, C.G., et al. *The English Presbyterians: from Elizabethan Puritanism to modern Unitarianism*. (George Allen & Unwin, 1968).
- Gordon, Alexander. *Heads of English Unitarian History, with appended essays on Baxter and Priestley*. (Philip Green, 1895).
- Smith, Leonard. *The Unitarians: a short history*. (Lensden Publishing, 2006).

Books of interest to Unitarian historians are listed at:

- Bibliography of British Unitarian History, with some references to the Commonwealth and Europe
  **www.unitarianhistory.org.uk/hsbib4.html**
  Includes Bibliography of Unitarian Congregations Which Have Existed Since 1800.

Some useful books on Unitarian history have been digitized at:

• The Unitarians: Document Library
  **www.unitarian.org.uk/document-library**

Many articles of interest have been published by denominational history societies. The Unitarian Historical Society **www.unitarian history.org.uk** has issued its *Transactions* since 1917. For a full list of its contents, see:

• Hill, Andrew M. *List of the articles and notes which have appeared in the Transactions 1917-2002 (Volumes 1-22).* Supplement to *Transactions of the Unitarian Historical Society* 23(1). 2003. This list is reproduced on the Society's website, where it is regularly updated.

## C. CONGREGATIONALISTS/INDEPENDENTS

The term 'Congregationalist' began to be applied to Independent churches in the late seventeenth century. The Independents owed their origin to a small minority of Elizabethan and Jacobean Puritans who questioned the parochial basis of Church of England membership and denied that the consent of a bishop was necessary before the Gospel could be proclaimed. For them, church membership was a privilege, not a right, and could only be given to those prepared to make an open avowal of their faith. Each individual congregation was responsible for its own government and the members' meeting was central. There was considered to be no scriptural basis for a close relationship between church and state.

The separatist movements of the Elizabethan and Jacobean periods were small, weak and persecuted, at times almost to extinction. It is unlikely, for example, that the Family of Love survived much later than c.1620,[2] although some former members may have joined the Quakers. Many separatists went into exile in the Low Countries. The earliest congregation which still survives is that at Llanvaches in Monmouthshire, founded in 1638.

The Independents flourished during the Civil War and Interregnum. Their numbers were smaller than the Presbyterians, but they had Cromwell on their side, and sufficient strength to prevent the development of a national Presbyterian system. Despite their separatist roots, some moderate Independents held parochial livings prior to the Restoration. It has been estimated that almost 200 of the clergy evicted from their livings in 1662 were Independents.

Given their theology, it is not surprising that the Independents created few national or regional organizations in the early days. As has been seen, they did join with the Presbyterians in the 'Happy Union' of the 1690s, but that quickly fell apart due to theological differences.

Independent churches were usually – but not always – resistant to the Unitarianism which swept through Presbyterian churches in the eighteenth century. Dissident Presbyterians frequently joined Independent congregations; indeed, many Congregational churches of the nineteenth century were formerly Presbyterian. The Methodist revival also encouraged new members in the late eighteenth century. Some of the churches founded by George Whitefield became Congregationalist, and the Countess of Huntingdon's Connexion (see below, pp.186–9) had close links with the Congregational Union. Congregationalism expanded considerably between the 1770s and 1851. Where there had been approximately 300 churches in 1772, there were over 3,000 in 1851.

At the end of the eighteenth century, under the influence of the evangelical revival, county unions were being formed (their records can often be found in local record offices). Their successful use of itinerant preachers on the Wesleyan model has already been noted. In 1831 the Congregational Union of Great Britain was established. Its history is outlined in:

- Peel, Albert. *These Hundred Years; a history of the Congregational Union of England and Wales, 1831-1931.* (Congregational Union of England and Wales, 1931).

The activities of a county union are described in:

• Powicke, Frederick James. *A History of the Cheshire County Union of Congregational Churches*. (Thomas Griffiths & Co., 1907).

Congregationalists, as already noted, came together with Presbyterians to form the United Reformed Church in 1972. A few Congregational churches which did not join in the union formed the Congregational Federation in 1972.

The central archives of the Congregational Union are now housed in the Congregational Library, administered with Dr. Williams's Library. For details, visit:

• Records of URC constituent churches
  **www.urc.org.uk/admin-and-resources/archives-and-record-keeping/2-general/862-constituent-churches-of-the-united-reformed-church.html**

### Records of Individual Congregational Churches

The prime sources of information on Congregational history, especially for local and family historians, are the records of particular congregations.

Great importance was attached to the founding church covenant, which can often be found at the beginning of church books, sometimes accompanied by a list of the founding members. The covenant may reveal how the church was originally formed. Church books contain the minutes of church meetings, which were central to the life of each church. They may also contain other peripheral material. For instance, the church book of Harpenden Congregational Church, 1870–1902, includes a printed list of subscribers to the Chapel Improvement Fund, 1879, recommendations of members transferring from other churches, a letter from Reverend William Price accepting the pastorate of the church, and a church membership roll.

Other documents from Harpenden relate to deacons' meetings and various other committees, church finance, church property, Sunday schools, membership, and pulpit notices (notice sheets). The latter, especially if associated with church magazines, may be invaluable sources for the history of particular churches.

*Ebenezer Congregational Chapel, St Davids.*

The range of topics which can be studied from the records of a particular church can be quite wide, for example, the call of ministers, membership, church discipline, the care of buildings, fundraising, and church organizations. Information about individuals can range from their acceptance into membership to their appointment as elders, from their non-attendance to their doctrinal deviations, from their drunkenness to certificates of their

*Holt (Wiltshire) Congregational Church.*

good standing on removal to other places. Some churches made provision for their poor; others were content to rely on the parish.
  For examples of early church books in print, see:

• Tibbutt, H.G., ed. *Some Early Nonconformist Church Books.* (Publications of the Bedfordshire Historical Record Society, 51, 1972).
• Tibbutt, H.G., ed. *The Minutes of the first Independent Church (now Bunyan Meeting) at Bedford 1656-1766.* (Publications of the Bedfordshire Historical Record Society, 55, 1976).

• Wordsworth, R.B. ed. *The Cockermouth Congregational Church Book (1651–c.1765)*. (Cumberland and Westmorland Antiquarian and Archaeological Society, Record Series, 21, 2012).

Sometimes, church officers were aware of the needs of future historians. In 1687, Axminster Independent Church resolved 'that this book of remembrance should be preserved, in which the most material matters . . . should be recorded and kept for those that may succeed in after times'. The result of this resolution has been published:

• Howard, K.W.H., ed. *The Axminster Ecclesia 1660-1698*. (Gospel Tidings Publications, 1976).

### Congregational Registers
The majority of Congregationalist registers of baptisms, marriages and burials were deposited with the Registrar General in the nineteenth century. They are now in The National Archives, in classes RG 4 and RG 8, and are available online (see above, pp.67–8). More recent registers have frequently been deposited in local record offices, although some remain in church safes. For a full listing of all surviving registers, see:

• Clifford, David J.H. *My Ancestors were Congregationalists in England and Wales: how can I find out more about them?*. (2nd ed. Society of Genealogists, 1997).

In addition to The National Archives' class lists, Congregationalist registers are also listed in the county volumes of the Society of Genealogists *National Index of Parish Registers*.

### Congregational Ministers and Laymen
Independency placed a high value on its full-time ministry, although pastors had less power than their Presbyterian counterparts. A paid minister was the norm, although a few churches could not afford one. The elaborate procedure involved in appointing ministers is usually minuted in detail. The appointment was always made by

individual congregations, but advice was often sought from other churches. Much information on Congregational ministers is given in the sources discussed above (and in Congregationalist periodicals – see below).

The archives of a number of northern ministerial training colleges are now held amongst the special collections of John Rylands Library in Manchester and may provide useful information concerning their students:

- Congregational College Archives
  **www.library.manchester.ac.uk/search-resources/guide-to-special-collections/atoz/congregational-college-archives**

Two biographical dictionaries of Congregationalists are also available:

- Peel, Albert. *The Congregational Two Hundred, 1530-1948.* (Independent Press, 1948).
- *Who's Who in Congregationalism.* (Shaw Publishing, 1933).

For Congregationalist Members of Parliament, see:

- Bebbington, David W. *Congregational Members of Parliament in the Nineteenth Century.* Occasional publication 1. (United Reformed Church History Society/Congregational History Society, 2007).

### Congregational Periodicals

The *Congregational Year Book* (1847–1972), succeeded by the *United Reformed Church Yearbook*, regularly listed churches and ministers, and included extensive obituaries. It also contained architectural descriptions of chapels. The 1855 *Yearbook* included a list of all Independent churches in England and Wales, including those which were not members of the Congregational Union. The 1901 edition included a consolidated listing of ministers who died in the nineteenth century. The *London Christian Instructor* (1818–25), continued by the *Congregational Magazine* (1826–45), also contained obituary notes, together with histories of many individual Independent and Baptist churches. Other denominational journals included the *Home Missionary Magazine* (1820–40) and the *Christian Witness* (1844–78). For a detailed listing, see the volume by Altholz (above, p.56).

For the journals of relevant historical societies, see above, pp.29 and 89. See also:

• *Congregational History Circle Magazine* (1979–2006). Continued by *Congregational History Society Magazine* (2007–).

### Missionary Activities

The London Missionary Society was an interdenominational body, but it was largely congregational in outlook and membership. Its main archives are held by SOAS and are listed on Aim25 **www.aim25.ac.uk**. They include much information on individual missionaries, including photographs. Letters received by the Society 1804–56 are held by Dr. Williams' Library. For other relevant collections, search 'London Missionary Society' at **www.mundus. ac.uk**.

Biographical notes on 1,482 missionaries are presented in:

• Sibree, James. *London Missionary Society: a register of Missionaries, Deputations, etc., from 1796 to 1923*. (London Missionary Society, 1923).

SOAS also holds a variety of other Congregational missionary material, including the archives of the Congregational Missionary Society. For the archives of the Council for World Mission, see:

• Porter, Andrew. 'The Council for World Mission and its archival legacy', *United Reformed Church Historical Society Transactions* 6(5), 1999, pp.346–61.

### Congregational Libraries and Record Offices.

The Congregational Library **http://conglib.co.uk** holds a portion of the library of the United Reformed Church History Society, and is now run in conjunction with Dr. Williams's Library. Its holdings are described in:

- Creasey, John. *The Congregational Library*. (Congregational Memorial Hall Trust, 1992).

and listed in:

- *A Catalogue of the Congregational Library, Memorial Hall, Farringdon Street, London E.C..* (1895). A second volume was published in 1910.

The library is the repository for Congregational Union records. These mainly consist of the minute books of its various committees and deal with the work of the ordained ministry, home and foreign missions, buildings, etc. Other records held include the archives of a number of Dissenting academies, and of Congregational organizations such as the Home Missionary Society 1819–79 (continued as the Congregational Church Aid and Home Missionary Society 1878–1924), the English Congregational Chapel Building Society 1853– 1932 (continued as the Church Building Committee 1933–64) and the Congregational Memorial Hall Trust. The Hall was erected in 1862 to commemorate the second centenary of the Great Ejection. Its archives include a list of subscribers.

**Research Guides**
A brief guide to Congregational sources is provided by:

- Tibbutt, H.G. 'Sources for Congregational church history', *Transactions of the Congregational Historical Society* 19, 1960–4, pp.33–8.

See also:

- Lea, John. 'Historical source materials on Congregationalism in nineteenth century Lancashire', *Journal of the United Reformed Church Historical Society* 1, 1973, pp.106–12.

Before writing up your research, you should read:

• Argent, Alan. 'Writing the history of Congregationalism 1900-2000', *Congregational History Magazine* 5(4), 2008, pp.224–49.

**Further Reading**
The standard denominational history is:

• Jones, R. Tudor. *Congregationalism in England 1662-1962.* (Independent Press, 1962).

For very early history, see:

• Tolmie, Murray. *The Triumph of the Saints: the separate churches of London, 1616-1649.* (Cambridge University Press, 1977).

A typescript bibliography of Congregational literature is available in the British Library, in the John Rylands University Library of Manchester, and possibly in other locations:

• Surman, Charles E. *A bibliography of Congregational church history, including numerous cognate Presbyterian/Unitarian records and a few Baptists.* (1947).

Many histories of individual East Anglian churches can be found in:

• Browne, John. *History of Congregationalism and memorials of the churches in Suffolk and Norfolk.* (Jarrold, 1877).

**D. BAPTISTS**
Baptists are defined by their insistence on the need for adult baptism and their opposition to infant baptism. Theirs was not a unified movement. General Baptists took an Arminian position, repudiating the Calvinistic doctrine of predestination and affirming that salvation was open to all. Particular Baptists took the opposite point of view. General Baptists tended towards a Presbyterian system of church government. Particular Baptists took a more Independent approach.

General and Particular Baptists had different origins and had little to do with each other until they formed the Baptist Union in 1891. Another group, the Seventh Day Baptists, worshipped on Saturdays rather than Sundays. They were few in number and will not be further noticed here. Strict Baptists emerged in the late eighteenth century from the Particular Baptist community. They took a more exclusive view of the sacraments and restricted communion to those who had undergone adult baptism by full immersion.

Both General and Particular Baptists founded a handful of churches before the Civil War. By 1660, both groups had over 100 churches each. A few Particular Baptists were ejected from parochial livings at the Restoration, but no General Baptists.

Like the Congregationalists, the Baptists experienced considerable growth in the late eighteenth and early nineteenth centuries. Josiah Thompson listed 402 churches in 1772 (see above, p.79). There were 2,789 in 1851. For two lists of early nineteenth-century Baptist chapels, see:

• *Two early nineteenth century lists of Baptist Churches, reprinted from the Baptist Magazine.*(Gage Postal Books, 1990).

**Associational Life**
The General Baptists initiated their General Assembly in 1654. Its minutes have been published:

• Whitley, W.T., ed. *Minutes of the General Assembly of the General Baptist churches in England, with kindred records.* (2 vols. Baptist Historical Society, 1909–10).

These minutes cover 1654–1728 and 1731–1811 and contain much useful information concerning ministers and churches. The Assembly deposited many of its records in Dr. Williams' Library.

The denomination was not free from theological controversy and many of its churches became Unitarian. Between 1697 and 1731, there was a rival General Baptist Association, with its own full minutes. Most of the anti-Unitarian churches left the General

Assembly in 1770 to form the New Connexion of General Baptists. Its minutes were regularly published.

The General Baptist Assembly still exists, but is Unitarian. The New Connexion merged with the Particular Baptists to form the Baptist Union of Great Britain (see below) in 1891. The minutes of the Baptist Union since 1812 are now held by the Angus Library at Regents Park College, Oxford (see below, pp.111–12). For its history, see:

• Payne, Ernest. *The Baptist Union: a Short History*. (Baptist Union of Great Britain and Ireland, 1958).

For the Associational history of the Particular Baptists, see:

• Breed, Geoffrey R. *Particular Baptists in Victorian England and their strict communion organizations*. (Baptist Historical Society, 2003).

Both General and Particular Baptists have had active regional associations since the seventeenth century. Their archives, especially those of the General Baptists, provide a great deal of information on matters such as the exchange of ministers, inspections of individual churches, correspondence, etc. The annual 'circular letters' sent by Associations to their member churches are particularly useful. They frequently include detailed statistics, the names of ministers and news from individual churches; they are usually more up to date than the equivalent information in the *Baptist Handbook* (see below). Many are in the Angus Library and the British Library; others can be identified in Copac and the *English Short Title Catalogue* (see above, p.27).

Early Association records of the Particular Baptists are printed in:

• Copson, S.L., ed. *Association Life of the Particular Baptists of Northern England 1699-1732*. (English Baptist records 3. Baptist Historical Society, 1991).
• White, B.R., ed. *Association Records of the Particular Baptists of England, Wales and Ireland to 1660*. (3 pts. Baptist Historical Society, 1971–7). Pt.1. South Wales and the Midlands. Pt.2. The West Country and Ireland. Pt.3. The Abingdon Association.

Other early Association records can be found in Dr. Williams's Library and in local record offices. The Particular Baptists' national association lapsed in the eighteenth century, until the Baptist Union was formed in 1813. In 1832 the Union was restructured in order to allow membership from General Baptist churches. The Strict Baptists did not join. Many are now *Gospel Standard* churches, having aligned themselves with the magazine of that name.

There are a number of useful studies of Baptist Associations in particular counties. These are likely to list member churches, identify church officers and may record published histories of particular chapels. See, for example:

- Buffard, Frank. *Kent and Sussex Baptist Associations*. (E. Vinson, 1964).
- Thornton, Elwyn. *The Northamptonshire Baptist Association*. (Carey Kingsgate Press, 1964).

### Local Baptist Church Records

The key unit of Baptist churchmanship was the local congregation. Many – but not all – churches had a paid minister and minutes are likely to contain much information on the pastorate. Elders and deacons also played important roles in church government and minutes record their election. All members were entitled to attend church meetings, which were held regularly and which made the decisions. All members were also expected to make regular financial contributions, which were often recorded in detail. Admittance to membership was much stricter than in Presbyterian churches. Applicants had to satisfy the whole congregation of the value of their spiritual experience. Formal consent to doctrine was not enough. Most had to undergo baptism by immersion.

Baptist church books include similar information to that found in the church books of other denominations. The confession of faith found at the commencement of a church book will identify a congregation's theological stance – repudiation of predestination for General Baptists, insistence on election for the Particulars. Baptists tended to emphasize the need for church harmony and consequently

*Bethel Baptist Church, Fishguard.*

their records minimize theological controversy and express regret when it occurred. However, there was a greater concern for discipline than in some other churches and minutes are full of information on the 'offences' of church members, such as drunkenness, fornication and disobedience to the church. Churches were also concerned to support members who had fallen on hard times and frequently paid rent and funeral expenses for their poor. In penal times, they paid fines and supported those who were persecuted for their faith. Church books frequently contain lists of members. Minutes of church and deacons' meetings are likely to record applications for baptism and for church membership. There may also be Sunday School registers, accounts, minutes of sub-committees and a variety of other documents. Registers of births, marriages and deaths were sometimes written in the same books as were used for minutes and other records. The archives of Baptist churches contain a mass of information on matters relating to the pastorate, finance and buildings.

Trust deeds are another important source; deeds provided legal title to chapel buildings and provide useful information on the early history of congregations. In addition to the works cited above (p.48), consult:

- Price, Seymour J. 'Baptist trust deeds', *Baptist Quarterly* New series 5, 1930–1, pp.102–10, 172–6 & 209–19.

Finding the records of particular congregations is not necessarily straightforward. Many have been deposited in local record offices, or in one of the Baptist institutions discussed below; others may be in the institutions listed in Chapter 2; others may still be with the church. Early records of particular congregations are printed in:

- Champion, L.G., ed. *The General Baptist Church of Berkhamstead, Chesham and Tring, 1712-1781.* (English Baptist records 1. Baptist Historical Society, 1985).
- *Church book: St. Andrews' Street Baptist Church, Cambridge 1720-1832.* (English Baptist records 2. Baptist Historical Society, 1991).
- Freeman, C.E., ed. 'A Luton Baptist minute book', *Publications of the Bedfordshire Historical Record Society* 25, 1947, pp.138–66.
- Whitley, W.B., ed. *The Church Books of Ford, or Cuddington and Amersham in the County of Bucks.* (Baptist Historical Society, 1912).

One of the earliest attempts to write the history of a Baptist church, written in the late seventeenth century, has recently been re-edited in:

- Hayden, Roger, ed. *The Records of a church of Christ in Bristol, 1640-1687.* (Bristol Record Society, 27, 1974).

### Baptist Registers
Baptist registers differ from those of other denominations, in that they do not record infant baptisms. Baptism required confession of

faith and the ensuing membership had to be approved by the church meeting. The rite was central, but it was for adults. The registers therefore record adult baptisms and cannot be used as a surrogate for birth registers. Nevertheless, many (but not all) Baptist churches did keep birth registers.

Marriage registers were rarely kept until the end of the nineteenth century, when churches were authorized to maintain their own registers as duplicates of the registers to be returned to district registrars. Some Baptist churches did, however, keep lists of marriages which had taken place elsewhere.

Many, but not all, Baptist registers were surrendered to the Registrar General in the nineteenth century and are now held by The National Archives (see above, pp.67–8). The county volumes of the *National Index of Parish Registers* provide lists of all surviving registers, whether surrendered or not. A full national listing is provided in:

• Breed, Geoffrey. *My Ancestors were Baptists: how can I find out more about them?* (4th rev. ed. Society of Genealogists, 2007).

Registers not only provide essential information for genealogists. They also provide the raw material for detailed analysis of a wide range of other matters. Caffyn's study of Sussex Baptist marriages lists all pre-1837 Sussex Baptist marriages and offers an example of what can be done by an enterprising local historian:

• Caffyn, John. *Sussex Believers: Baptist marriage in the 17th and 18th centuries*. (Churchman, 1988).

### Baptist Ministers

Some sources for Baptist ministers have already been mentioned. The manuscripts of John Evans and Josiah Thompson noted above (p.79) mention many Baptists. A list compiled by Rev. John Collett Ryland, c.1750, appears in:

• 'Baptist ministers in England about 1750', *Baptist Historical Society Transactions* 6, 1919, pp.138–57.

A list based on Ryland's work, but with additions made in 1763, appears in:

• Ivimey, Joseph. *A History of the English Baptists*. (Isaac Taylor Hinton, 1830), vol. 4, pp.13–21.

Various lists of ministers appear in the *Baptist Annual Register* (1790–1802). Similar listings appear in the 1811, 1823, 1827, 1831, 1835 and 1851–60 issues of the *Baptist Magazine*.

Over 7,000 Baptist ministers are identified at:

• Baptist Pastors and Chapels database
  **www.strictbaptisthistory.org.uk/dbsearch/search.htm**

See also:

• 'An index to notable Baptists whose careers began within the British Empire before 1850', *Transactions of the Baptist Historical Society* 7, 1921, pp.182–239.

Obituaries are another useful source of information. They can be found in many periodicals. The Baptist Historical Society **www. baptisthistory.org.uk** maintains an Index of Baptist Ministers' Obituaries.

A contemporary biographical dictionary was published in 1933:

• *The Baptists Who's Who*. (Shaw Publishing, 1933).

The Particular Baptist Fund was established in 1717 to assist Baptist ministers; their education was seen as a vital part of the Fund's work. Its minutes record the names of ministers, churches and colleges helped by the Fund and are an important source of Baptist history. They are held by the Angus Library. For the history of the Fund, visit:

• The Particular Baptist Fund
  **www.pbfund.org.uk**

## Baptist Missionary Records

Baptist missionary activity has been channelled through the Baptist Missionary Society (BMS) since it was founded in 1792. The archives of the Society are held by the Angus Library (see below), although related material is held by many other record offices. The holdings include committee minutes from 1792, together with the correspondence, diaries and reports from both overseas missionaries and the officers of the Society. These provide much personal information on missionaries, but are also important for studying a wide range of other topics, ranging from Hinduism to exploration, from the Boxer Rebellion to botany. For full details, search 'Baptist Missionary Society' at Mundus **www.mundus.ac.uk**. See also:

- BMS: Our Heritage
  **www.bmsworldmission.org/heritage**

*Mission house and school of the Baptist Missionary Society at Amboises Bay, Cameroons.*

Many BMS archives have been microfilmed by the Southern Baptist Historical Society, and the films can be purchased. For a full list of microfilms available, visit:

• Southern Baptist Historical Society Finding Aids
  **www.sbhla.org/finding_aids.asp**
  Search 'Baptist Missionary Society'.

For a detailed history of Baptist missionary endeavours, see:

• Stanley, Brian. *The History of the Baptist Missionary Society, 1792-1992*. (T. & T. Clark, 1992).

William Carey was one of the founders of the Baptist Missionary Society. For a huge amount of information about contemporary Baptists, a digital library of his writings, and an extensive bibliography, visit:

• Center for Study of the Life and Work of William Carey, D.D. (1761–1834)
  **www.wmcarey.edu/carey**

**Baptist Periodicals**
A wide variety of Baptist periodicals are available. Many are listed by Altholz (above, p.56), but a full listing of specifically Baptist journals is provided by:

• Taylor, Rosemary. 'English Baptist periodicals, 1790-1865', *Baptist Quarterly* 27(2), 1977, pp.50–82.

The aim of the *General Baptist Repository* (1802–59) was to make the scattered churches of the denomination better acquainted with each other. It was succeeded by the *General Baptist Magazine* (1860–91) *The Baptist Magazine* (1809–1904) was a semi-official Particular Baptist organ.

The Baptist Union has published an annual handbook since 1832, under various titles: *Account of the proceedings of the annual sessions of the Baptist Union* (1832–44), *The Baptist Manual* (1845–59), the *Baptist Handbook* (1860–1972) and the *Baptist Union Directory* (1978– ). This includes lists of member churches and their ministers, together with obituaries (see above for an index); it also includes a brief outline of Baptist history. Lists of Particular Baptist congregations were also occasionally published in *The Baptist Magazine* (see above), which also published alphabetical lists of ministers between 1851 and 1860. The General Baptists' New Connexion issued the *General Baptist Yearbook* (1868–91).

For an earlier periodical which included lists of Baptist congregations, see:

• *Baptist Annual Register*, ed. John Rippon. (4 vols. 1790–1802). This is now available online at the Hathi Trust **www.hathitrust.org/home** and elsewhere.

Personal names in magazines from the Strict Baptist denomination are indexed in:

• Strict Baptist Personal Names database **www.strictbaptisthistory.org.uk/pnsearch/searchpn.htm**

An index to *The Baptist Magazine* is available to members of the Society of Genealogists at:

• What's on SoG Data Online? **www.sog.org.uk/search-records/whats-on-sog-data-online**

### Baptist Libraries and Record Offices

**The Angus Library**, at Oxford's Regent's Park College, is the principal repository of Baptist records. It holds the archives of the Baptist Union and the Baptist Missionary Society, together with the library of the Baptist Historical Society and papers from a variety of other Baptist organizations. Some Association and chapel records are held, although the majority of the latter are deposited in local record offices, if they are not still with the church. The library also holds the archives of Regents Park College, which include much information on past students who entered the ministry. See:

- The Angus Library and Archive
  **http://theangus.rpc.ox.ac.uk**
  The family history page on this site has details of over 5,000 Baptist missionaries.

The library's catalogue is now incorporated in Oxford University's Bodleian Library catalogue at **http://solo.bodleian.ox.ac.uk**. A printed catalogue published in 1908 may also be useful:

- *Catalogue of the books, pamphlets & manuscripts in the Angus Library at Regent's Park College, London.* (Kingsgate Press, 1908).

**The Baptist Historical Society** aims to help everyone interested in Baptist history; its website has useful information for all researchers and also lists the Society's publications. Its library is now held in the Angus Library (see above). For information on the Society, visit:

- Baptist Historical Society
  **www.baptisthistory.org.uk**

The library and archives of **Bristol Baptist College** hold much material on Baptist and Dissenting history, including information about all its former students, portraits of former staff and other Baptist historical ephemera. Visit:

- Bristol Baptist College Library and Archives
  **www.bristol-baptist.ac.uk/further-information/library-and-archives**

**The Strict Baptist Historical Society** has a library and has issued many publications. Its website has much useful information:

• Strict Baptist Historical Society
  **www.strictbaptisthistory.org.uk/index.htm**

The **Gospel Standard Baptist Library** caters for Strict Baptist churches, some of whom have deposited records. For details including a listing of the church records held, see:

• Gospel Standard Baptist Library
  **www.gospelstandard.org.uk/GS-Library**

The archives of a number of northern Baptist institutions, including the Baptist Building Fund Liverpool Auxiliary, Lancashire and Cheshire Association of Baptist Churches, Lancashire and Cheshire Baptist Women's League, Bury and Rossendale District Baptist Lay Preachers' Association, Manchester District Baptist Union and Lancashire and Cheshire Baptist Women's Federation, are held by the **John Rylands' Library** amongst the

• Northern Baptist College Archive
  **www.library.manchester.ac.uk/search-resources/guide-to-special-collections/atoz/northern-baptist-college-archive**

**Regent's Park College**, see Angus Library.

Like other denominational colleges, **Spurgeon's College** archives contain much information about past students, who are now listed in an off-line database. Many photographs are held. Much material related to the College's founder is held in the C.H. Spurgeon Archive and Heritage Room.

• Spurgeon's College: The Library
  **www.spurgeons.ac.uk/why/library**

**Further Reading**
The essential guide to Baptist historical sources (with worldwide – especially American – coverage) is:

*Spurgeon preaching at Surrey Music Hall.*

- Mills, S.J. *Probing the Past: a toolbox for Baptist historical research.* (Baptist Historical Society, 2009).

See also:

- Richards, Thomas. 'Some disregarded sources of Baptist history', *Baptist Quarterly* New Series, 17(8) 1958, pp.362–79.

A number of works offer general advice on writing Baptist history. See:

- Hayden, Roger. 'Writing the history of a local Baptist church', *Baptist Quarterly* New Series 22(8), 1968, pp.409–17.
- Nuttall, Geoffrey F. 'The task of a Baptist historian', *Baptist Quarterly* New Series 22, 1967–8, pp.398–408 & 428.
- Strict Baptist Historical Society: Writing your Church or Chapel History
  **www.strictbaptisthistory.org.uk/_private/writing.htm**

• White, B.R. *Writing Baptist History*. Baptist Union, 1965.

A useful basic reference work (with a strong American bias) is provided by:

• Brackney, William H. *Historical Dictionary of Baptists*. (Scarecrow Press, 1999).

There are many general historical accounts. Some more recent volumes include:

• Briggs, J.H.Y. *The English Baptists of the Nineteenth Century*. (Baptist Historical Society, 1994).
• Brown, Raymond. *The English Baptists of the Eighteenth Century*. (Baptist Historical Society, 1986).
• Hayden, Roger. *English Baptist History and Heritage*. (2nd ed. Baptist Union, 2005).
• Randall, Ian M. *The English Baptists of the Twentieth Century*. (Baptist Historical Society, 2005).
• Rinaldi, Frank. *The Tribe of Dan: The New Connexion of General Baptists 1770-1891: a Study in the Transition from Revival Movement to Established Denomination*. (Paternoster Press, 2008).
• Shepherd, Peter. *The Making of a Modern Denomination: John Howard Shakespeare and the English Baptists 1898-1924*. (Paternoster Press, 2001).
• White, B.R. *The English Baptists of the 17th Century*. (Rev. ed. Baptist Historical Society, 1994).
• Whitley, William Thomas. *A History of British Baptists*. (2nd ed. Kingsgate Press, 1932).
• Wright, Stephen. *The Early English Baptists, 1603–1649*. (Boydell & Brewer, 2006).

Two works may be cited as representative of a number of useful regional histories:

• *Baptists in Yorkshire, Lancashire, Cheshire Cumberland*. (Kingsgate Press for the Baptist Historical Society, 1913).

- Whitley, W.T. *Baptists of North West England 1649-1913.* (Kingsgate Press, 1913).

For Strict Baptists, see:

- Chambers, Ralph F., et al. *The Strict Baptist Chapels of England.* (5 vols. Strict Baptist Historical Society, 1952–68). Vol.1: The Chapels of Surrey and Hampshire. Vol. 2: The Chapels of Sussex. Vol. 3: The Chapels of Kent. Vol. 4: The Chapels of the Industrial Midlands, including Worcestershire, Shropshire, Staffordshire, Warwickshire, Leicestershire, Northamptonshire, Huntingdonshire, Rutland, and South-West Lincolnshire. Vol. 5: The Chapels of Wiltshire and the West, including Cornwall, Devon, Dorset, Glamorgan, Gloucestershire, Somerset and Wiltshire. Typescripts for unpublished further volumes are in the Angus Library.
- Dix, Kenneth. *Strict and Particular: English Strict and Particular Baptists in the nineteenth century.* (Baptist Historical Society, for the Strict Baptist Historical Society, 2001).
- Naylor, P. *Picking up a Pin for the Lord: English Particular Baptists from 1688 to the early nineteenth century.* (Grace Publications, 1992).

For the Welsh Baptists, see:

- Bassett T.M. *The Welsh Baptists.* (Ilston House, 1977).

There are many local studies, most of which cannot be listed here. Two works on Oxford Baptists are models of the genre. Kreitzer provides detailed biographies of some of the men who came together to form the local church, together with extensive transcripts of seventeenth-century sources:

- Kreitzer, Larry J. *Seditious Sectaryes: The Baptist Conventiclers of Oxford, 1641-1691.* (2 vols. Paternoster Press, 2006).

The later history of Oxford Baptists is recounted in a collection of essays:

• Chadwick, R.E., ed. *A Protestant Catholic Church of Christ: essays on the history and life of New Road Baptist Church, Oxford*. (The Church, 2003).

Another excellent local study is provided by:

• Binfield, Clyde. *Pastors and People: the biography of a Baptist church, Queen's Road, Coventry*. (The Church, 1984).

Many useful articles are published in:

• *Transactions of the Baptist Historical Society*. (1908–21). Continued by the *Baptist Quarterly*. (1923– ). Digitized images are available at **www.biblicalstudies.org.uk**.

The history of an important fund is outlined in:

• Price, Seymour James. *A Popular History of the Baptist Building Fund; the centenary volume, 1824-1924*. (Kingsgate Press, 1927). This includes a list of grants made to individual churches.

A variety of Baptist documents can be found on two internet sites:

• Baptist History Homepage: A Source for Original Baptist Documents
  **http://baptisthistoryhomepage.com/**
• The Reformed Reader: committed to Historic Baptist Beliefs
  **www.reformedreader.org**

Many other works can be identified by consulting Baptist bibliographies:

• Starr, Edward C. *A Baptist bibliography, being a register of printed material by and about Baptists; including works written against the*

*Baptists.* (25 vols. Judson Press for the Samuel Colgate Baptist Historical Collection, 1947–76). Also available at **www.baptistheritage.com/starr-baptist-bibliography.**

- Whitley, W.T. *A Baptist bibliography: being a register of the chief materials for Baptist history, whether in manuscript or in print, preserved in Great Britain, Ireland and the colonies.* (2 vols. Kingsgate Press, 1916–22. Reprinted 1985).

# Chapter 4

# THE QUAKERS

The British have a habit of adopting names which were originally given contemptuously by their opponents. When Kaiser Wilhelm II described the British Army in the First World War as a contemptible little army, he did not expect them to become the 'Old Contemptibles'. Likewise, 'Methodists' was the derisive name given to Wesleyans by their opponents at Oxford, and 'Quakers' was the scornful term used to describe members of the Society of Friends. The term derived from the trembling and shaking which characterised their meetings in the early days.

Quakerism, like the 'Three Denominations' discussed in the previous chapter, originated out of the ferment created by the English Civil War. The Friends, as they prefer to be known, took Continental Anabaptism to its logical conclusion by completely denying the validity of formalism in religion. Even baptism was rejected. Quakers rejected formal church services, set creeds and paid ministers or priests. They emphasized the 'inner voice' and the possibility of direct communication with God, practising silence in their worship and downgrading the authority of scripture.

Even before the restoration of Charles II in 1660, the Quakers were a persecuted minority. Their 'rude and unchristian disturbance' of church services, their scorn of what they considered to be a 'hireling ministry', their refusal to pay tithes, and their studied rudeness in refusing to remove their hats in deference to magistrates, did not endear them to the Cromwellian authorities. After the Restoration, the Cavaliers were even more hostile. They saw the Quakers as a very serious threat to their regime and imposed heavy penalties on them. In consequence, the 'sufferings' of Quakers during the late Stuart period are very well documented (see below, pp.131–4).

Friends did, however, have an advocate at Charles II's court. William Penn, the son of a distinguished admiral, fearlessly defended them. In 1681, Charles II granted him the proprietorship of a large tract of land in North America. Pennsylvania became a Quaker colony and attracted many persecuted Friends. Its capital, Philadelphia, had 2,500 inhabitants within two years of its foundation.

At the same time as Pennsylvania was being founded, the worst rigours of persecution in England were being dismantled. The Declarations of Indulgence of 1672 and 1687 foreshadowed the Toleration Act of 1689. The Affirmation Act of 1696, amended in 1727, removed another grievance. Quakers were to be tolerated, although they continued to be liable to pay tithes and to serve in the Militia. They were still excluded from public office and the Universities.

These disabilities caused Quakers to turn to business. Their frugality and their reputation for honesty encouraged business success. Some of the leading figures in the Industrial Revolution were Quakers. Lloyds Bank still survives as a testimony to eighteenth-century Quaker integrity. Prosperity meant that it was possible for Quakers to develop a range of charitable organizations, such as schools and hospitals, and to fund campaigns on issues such as the state of prisons and the slave trade.

Nevertheless, Quaker numbers declined throughout the eighteenth and nineteenth centuries. In the early eighteenth century, between 80 per cent and 90 per cent of Quakers were the children of members.[1] Quaker 'discipline' discouraged many from continuing as Friends – especially those who had been born into the denomination and had 'birthright' membership. The requirements for continued membership of the Society became more rigorous. It became virtually impossible to 'marry out' of the Society without being 'disowned'. It is ironic that the heirs of an ecstatic mysticism were so dismissive of the emotionalism of evangelical religion. Late eighteenth-century Methodists, and other Dissenters, gained many adherents from disgruntled (and sometimes disowned) Quakers. Nevertheless, the evangelical revival led by the Wesleys also had a positive impact within the Society. Throughout the nineteenth century there was a tension between the more evangelical wing of the Society and the more conservative Quietists, who sought to preserve the Society's traditions of speech and dress.

The causes of decline amongst Friends were identified by J.S. Rowntree when he entered a competition for the best essay on the subject in 1858. He decried some of the Puritanical attitudes of contemporary Quakers, attacked the high level of disownments amongst those who married outside of the Society, and argued for the importance of Quaker education. His comments were taken on board and many reforms were instituted in the following decades. Schools were founded, missionaries were sent out and the eighteenth-century Quietist emphasis on humanitarian activity was developed.

## QUAKER ORGANIZATION

The structure of the Society of Friends is not easy to describe, since the relationships and functions of the different 'Meetings' varied, not only over time, but also in different places. The names of Meetings were not always used consistently, especially where they regularly met in several different locations. For example, documents which record the business of the Faringdon Monthly Meeting and the Abingdon Monthly Meeting are actually recording the different venues of the same Monthly Meeting. The boundaries of Meetings were also fluid. These became more stable after 1836, as a result of the fact that thereafter the Registrar General needed to know the areas for which Monthly Meeting registrars took responsibility.

Broadly, the London Yearly Meeting was at the apex of the Society. As its name suggests, it met in London – but it was not composed primarily of London Friends. Rather, it was a Meeting of representatives from all the Quarterly Meetings, together with acknowledged ministers, elders and correspondents. In 1837, there were twenty-six Quarterly Meetings in existence, each of them responsible for ensuring that the *Advices* issued by the London Yearly

Meeting were implemented and that Friends' discipline was properly maintained by each Monthly Meeting within their area.

Monthly Meetings were the primary forum for the administration of church affairs and for the exercise of the discipline. They were composed of representatives of the Preparative Meeting in their area. Each Monthly Meeting was responsible for a number of Preparative Meetings, which in turn were usually formed by single Particular Meetings (i.e. congregations), although occasionally two or three Particular Meetings might come together in a single Preparative Meeting. Particular Meetings were sometimes quite small. Friends were not encumbered by a paid ministry and their Meetings could therefore be smaller than the congregations of other denominations.

There were many variations from this structure, both over time and between regions. In some areas, the pressure of business was such that 'Two Week Meetings' were required. In Bristol, the Men's Meeting acted as both Monthly and Quarterly Meetings and sent its own representatives to London Yearly Meeting. Its minutes have been published:

- Mortimer, Russell, ed. *Minute Book of the Men's Meeting of the Society of Friends in Bristol, 1667-1686.* (Bristol Record Society 26, 1970). This is continued for 1686–1704 in 30, 1977.

For a good introduction to the structure of Friends' Meetings, consult:

- Mortimer, Jean. 'Meetings for church affairs within Britain Yearly Meeting', *Quaker Connections* 11, 1997, pp.9–17; 12, 1997, pp.7–13.

Despite their denial of the need for a paid priestly hierarchy and their belief that anyone could be used in ministry, Quakers did acknowledge that some Friends had a particular 'gift in the ministry'. Such 'ministers' received 'acknowledgement' as 'publick Friends' (although this ceased in 1924). Sometimes 'liberations' of ministers to 'travel in the ministry' can be found in Quaker minutes. Travelling ministers helped bind the Society together.[2]

'Elders' were also appointed. Their role was advisory; they were closely involved in disciplinary matters. Ministers and elders met together in various Meetings of their own. They made a major contribution to establishing a strong organizational structure for the Society. Each Meeting also appointed its own clerk, who was responsible for taking minutes and keeping records. Historians are entirely dependent on their efficiency.

### Particular and Preparative Meetings and their Records

The Particular Meeting was, until 1966, the assembly in which Quakers normally met for worship. It also met for administrative purposes once a month in a Preparative Meeting. As its name suggests, the primary function of the Preparative Meeting was to prepare for the Monthly Meeting. It did this by answering queries issued by the Monthly Meeting. These answers were recorded in minute books, which form a valuable resource for researchers. Monthly Meetings relied on the information which Preparative Meetings were able to collect. The latter could be much better informed on particular cases.

Preparative Meetings also managed the affairs of their own Meetings. In most cases, much of the work was done by Monthly Meetings, but sometimes Preparative Meeting had wider responsibilities for finance and property, and their minutes are therefore fuller. Records of such Meetings may include account books and other records. Confusingly, they may be referred to as Monthly Meetings. For the minutes of one such meeting, see:

• Mortimer, Jean, & Mortimer, Russell, eds. *Leeds Friends' Minute Book, 1692 to 1712*. (Yorkshire Archaeological Society Record series 139, 1980).

Until the nineteenth century, women met separately. Women's meetings sometimes exercised pastoral responsibilities, although they could be overruled by Men's meetings. Their minutes might record relief activities, such as gifts of fuel or money to those who had fallen on hard times. Quakers always tried to ensure that their members were looked after.

Preparative Meetings were also involved in administering the procedures for marriage. Couples had to inform their Preparative Meeting of their intention to marry, before following the procedures at Monthly Meetings outlined below. Some Preparative Meetings maintained their own registers of births, marriages and deaths.

### Monthly Meetings and their Records
Membership, discipline, finance and property were amongst the responsibilities of the Monthly Meetings,[3] which supervised perhaps four to seven Preparative Meetings. Again, these were divided into Men's and Women's Meetings, the women often taking responsibility for pastoral work and poor relief. Women's Meetings tended to be less busy, with more time for worship and reflection.

The Monthly Meeting registered births, marriages and deaths. It kept membership registers and recorded the removal and settlement of Friends. It was involved in educational work, concerned itself with the relief of the poor, and arranged apprenticeships. It recorded the 'sufferings' of Friends, disowned those who had broken Society rules, and perhaps reinstated them. It recognized 'publick friends', that is, those who were 'acknowledged' as ministers.

Minutes of Monthly Meetings frequently supply much detailed information about church affairs. So does their correspondence. Sometimes, draft minutes survive and can be compared with the finished version. Minutes were particularly important to Quakers and clerks had to be very careful to reflect the sense of the meetings they recorded.

A variety of other records survive. Accounts and other financial records provide information about financial transactions, often revealing both the names of subscribers and the recipients of relief. Deeds record property. Membership registers provide lists of members. Books of Sufferings record the consequences of Society membership for those who were persecuted. Epistles exchanged with the London Yearly Meeting and other meetings contained religious exhortations and practical advice on a wide range of matters; they enable us to track the state of the Society. Of course, not every Meeting kept all these records and the record keeping skills of Meeting Clerks varied. In general, however, surviving records of Monthly Meetings are more extensive and detailed than the records of other denominations.

The minutes of a number of Monthly Meetings have been published by record societies. See, for example:

- Brace, Harold W., ed. *The First Minute Book of the Gainsborough Monthly Meeting of the Society of Friends, 1669-1719.* 2 vols. (Lincoln Record Society 38, 40 & 44, 1948–51).
- Snell, Beatrice Saxon, ed. *The Minute Book of the Monthly Meeting of the Society of Friends for the Upperside of Buckinghamshire, 1669-1690.* (Buckinghamshire Archaeological Society Records Branch, 1, 1937). Digitized at **www.bucksrecsoc.org.uk**.

A number of transcripts of Monthly Meeting minutes are held in Friends House Library. These (and printed editions) are mostly confined to the late seventeenth and early eighteenth centuries.

### Quarterly Meetings and their Records

Originally, there was a Quarterly Meeting for every English county. In the late eighteenth and nineteenth centuries a number were amalgamated, so that by 1966 (when they lost most of their business functions and were re-named 'General Meetings') there were only eighteen.

Quarterly Meetings were composed of representatives from the Monthly Meetings in their area. The division of responsibilities between Monthly and Quarterly Meetings was often blurred, especially before 1700. However, Quarterly Meetings gradually assumed the role of an appeal court for disputed matters, especially in relationship to disownments. They issued queries to Monthly Meetings and took action if 'exceptions' were reported by them. They sent representatives to London Yearly Meeting, passed on recommendations from Monthly Meetings to the Yearly Meeting, and tried to ensure that directives issued by the Yearly Meeting were implemented by Monthly Meetings. The minutes of the Somerset Quarterly Meeting are transcribed in:

• Morland, Stephen C., ed. *The Somersetshire Quarterly Meeting of the Society of Friends, 1668-1699.* (Somerset Record Society 75, 1978).

An index to the minutes of London and Middlesex Quarterly Meeting, 1671–1868, is available at Friends House Library.

### London Yearly Meeting

The London Yearly Meeting oversaw the Society of Friends. It should not be confused with the many Yearly Meetings held for worship and other purposes, nor with the Friends who lived in London. Prior to 1905, it always met in London. In 1995, it was renamed 'Britain Yearly Meeting'. Its purpose was – and is – to exercise oversight over the affairs of the Society. It was initially composed of 'ministering' Friends, but, since 1678, has been representative in character. Each Quarterly Meeting sent representatives, as did Friends in Scotland and Ireland; there was also representation from the Meeting for Sufferings and links with overseas Friends. Acknowledged ministers might also attend. Increasingly, other Friends also attended. In 1861, the Meeting was opened to all male Friends. There was a separate Women's Meeting until 1907. A list of 6,000 male representatives, 1668–1861, is held by Friends House Library.

The London Yearly Meeting exercised a considerable degree of authority in the life of the Society of Friends. It regularly sent out 'summaries' of its thinking on a wide range of topics – and it expected Meetings lower in the hierarchy to enforce its directives. Topics such as the pagan names of days and months, the keeping of records, the use of 'thee' in addressing people, and simplicity of lifestyle, were all dealt with in its 'summaries' and its annual epistles. Its queries, which developed into routine, nevertheless threw a searching spotlight on the activities of the Society as a whole. They ceased in 1875.

The minutes of the London Yearly Meeting normally included the names of representatives, accounts of sufferings, answers to queries, epistles from other Yearly Meetings, consideration of the state of the Society, and propositions from Quarterly Meetings. It also received appeals from individuals against the decisions of Quarterly and Monthly meetings, but normally did not minute them. A working index to the minutes, 1672–1856, is available at Friends House Library (see below), as are the minutes themselves. Other records include 'testimonies concerning ministers deceased', records of sufferings, and epistles exchanged with other Yearly Meetings.

## MEMBERSHIP RECORDS

Membership was the responsibility of Monthly Meetings, and their records must be consulted in order to trace individual members. In the early days, there was no formal definition of membership. Rather, it was based on 'convincement' and on the continuing evidence of Quaker-like behaviour. Unlike other denominations, Friends did not baptise their converts; instead, they relied on 'convincements' for new members. Formal records of 'convincements' were not kept prior to the mid-eighteenth century. The researcher must rely on other evidence in minutes and correspondence to establish when a particular member was 'convinced'. Such evidence might include, for example, applications to marry, appointment to a particular duty, the grant of poor relief or notice of removal. The children of Friends were automatically eligible for 'birthright' membership.

Few membership registers pre-date 1812, when the London Yearly Meeting minuted that 'considerable advantage would arise from each Monthly Meeting keeping an alphabetical list of its members and examining such list at least once in the year'. Not all Meetings complied and the subject was taken up again in 1837.

The introduction of civil registration meant that the Quakers had to reform their registration procedures (see below, pp.137–8). As part of that reform, every Monthly Meeting was directed to keep a membership register, which was compiled in a printed book. Birth and death notes (see below), which had formerly been used in registration procedures, were henceforth to be used to keep the membership register up to date.

A removal certificate was normally issued by Monthly Meetings when a Friend moved house. It would be sent directly by the clerk of the old Monthly Meeting to the clerk of the new Monthly Meeting. Before this was done, the conduct of the Friend would be investigated. If he was a minister or elder, this would be noted. The names of wives and children were noted on certificates, which were signed by at least three Friends besides the clerk of the Meeting. Insolvents were not granted certificates, nor were recent recipients of poor relief, or members who had been disowned. If there were complications, it might take months for a certificate to be issued. Certificates established the credentials of Friends with their new Monthly Meeting, who would arrange for them to be visited in their new home. Outgoing certificates began to be recorded by Monthly Meetings in the mid-eighteenth century. Incoming certificates were not necessarily recorded, but were sometimes kept on file. In the nineteenth century, some Monthly Meetings kept a separate removal certificate book. These records provide an invaluable and extensive source of evidence for geographical mobility, particularly useful for tracking the process of urbanization during the Industrial Revolution. They may also be useful for tracing emigration to North America. Those relating to Philadelphia are recorded in:

• Myers, Albert Cook, ed. *Quaker Arrivals at Philadelphia, 1682-1750, being a list of certificates of removal received at Philadelphia Monthly Meeting of Friends.* (Philadelphia: Ferris & Leach, 1902).

## DISOWNMENTS

Many Meetings lost members by disownment. Indeed, disownments were probably a major reason for the Society's decline during the eighteenth and nineteenth centuries. It was equivalent to the penalty of excommunication in the Church of England. Friends who were disowned ceased to be regarded as Friends. Like excommunication, disownment became an increasingly poor means of enforcing discipline. The rigidity of Quaker 'discipline', especially in matters of marriage, caused many to leave the Society. Quakers, like other Christians, were likely to object to drunkenness, commercial dishonesty (sometimes including bankruptcy) and sexual laxity. There were a variety of other reasons for disownment specific to the Quakers. They objected to members participating in religious ceremonies performed by priests or ministers of other denominations. In particular, they would not allow members to marry non-Friends (especially before a priest). Members who paid tithes, or joined the Militia, were likely to be disowned.

The procedure for disownment was slow. Offenders were interviewed and repentance was sought repeatedly. Only if all else failed were members disowned. Everything was recorded, especially in more recent times. The offender might be given a 'testimony of denial' or 'disownment', which would be read out to the Meeting and copied into its minute book. The disowned might subsequently be reinstated. Disownments and reinstatements are recorded in Monthly Meeting minutes.

## MARRIAGE

Monthly Meetings had oversight and effective control of Quaker marriages. In the early days, Quakers were fortunate that, despite ecclesiastical censure, 'irregular' marriages were recognized by the common law. They could therefore legally marry without a church ceremony and their marriages were accepted as valid. Detailed procedures for marriage were developed and standardized in 1753. Those procedures have left extensive records. It has been estimated that between a quarter and a third of the entries in Monthly Meeting minute books relate to marriage procedure. After giving notice to their Preparative Meetings, Quakers were expected to make a public declaration of their intention to marry at two or three successive Monthly Meetings. Their fitness to marry would be thoroughly investigated. Marriage to non-Quakers was discouraged. Couples could not be related to each other (and the Quaker definition of relationship was much wider than that of the Church of England); they had to be free of any prior commitment and they had to avoid an 'over-hasty' second marriage. Only after investigations had been completed would the Monthly Meeting formally 'liberate' couples to marry. Liberations were to the Quakers what banns were to Anglicans, but were much more difficult to obtain. They were recorded in Monthly Meeting minutes, as were the preliminary proceedings. The minutes are therefore likely to give more information than is contained in the actual marriage registers (for these, see below, pp.134–8). Having been liberated, the couple were then expected to declare their commitment in a public worship meeting. The marriage could then take place.

Quakers could not countenance members who took their vows before a priest. Whilst marriage to a non-member was not in itself a disownable offence, marriage in the Church of England was. And, after 1754, there was no legal alternative open to those who were not allowed to marry in the Meeting House. Hardwicke's Marriage Act of the previous year specified that, in future, only members of the Society could marry in Quaker meeting houses.

The requirements for Quaker marriage to take place were irksome, liberations could not always be secured, and marriage by a Church of England priest was relatively easy. After 1837, marriage by a registrar was not frowned on quite as much as marriage by a priest, but even so, Friends considered marriage to be a religious ordinance, not a civil one. It was not until 1859 that the law allowed marriage with a non-Friend to take place in a meeting house, and not until 1872 that anyone could marry there. Even then, until c.1900, those who 'married out' were frequently disowned by the Society. Such disownments were recorded in Monthly Meeting minutes.

For a full discussion of Quaker marriage, including a list of 'legislation affecting Quaker marriage', see:

• Milligan, Edward. *Quaker Marriage*. (Quaker Tapestry Scheme, 1994).

See also:

• Mortimer, R.S. 'Marriage discipline in early Friends: a study in church administration illustrated from Bristol records', *Journal of the Friends Historical Society* 48, 1956–8, pp.175–95.

## SUFFERINGS

The Establishment in late seventeenth and early eighteenth century English society considered the Quakers to be insufferable. They refused to swear oaths or attend the established church, would not pay tithes, undertake service in the Militia, or even pay for a substitute. They sometimes travelled on Sundays. Quaker teachers taught without a licence from the bishop; Quaker tradesmen opened for business on Sundays and other holy days. The Conventicle Act forbade meetings of five or more people for worship – a law that the Quakers regularly flouted. Their behaviour went against the grain of the society in which early Quakers lived. Consequently, they suffered persecution. Informers against them could be rewarded by Quarter Sessions. About 15,000 were fined, imprisoned, or transported for refusal to take the oath of supremacy and allegiance under Charles II.[4] Even after the Toleration Act of 1689, they could still be distrained upon for failure to pay tithes, and penalised for refusal to serve in the Militia. But if they gave way to the demands of the 'world', their behaviour might be questioned by other Friends and they could be 'disowned' by the Society.

The 'Sufferings' of Quakers who were prosecuted by the authorities were recorded in detail by the Meeting for Sufferings, which met weekly from 1676 to deal with cases from throughout the country. They kept the *Great Books of Sufferings*, which are now held at Friends House Library and comprise forty-four volumes. These include the returns of Sufferings made by Quarterly Meetings from 1650 to 1856. It was not until 1873 that Suffering records were officially discontinued. Joseph Besse published abstracts from the *Great Books* in 1753. If an individual is mentioned in these abstracts, the probability is that more information will be found in the *Great Books*. A facsimile reprint of Besse's book has recently been issued in a series of volumes:

• Besse, Joseph. *Sufferings of early Quakers in Yorkshire, 1652-1690: facsimile of part of the 1753 edition*, with new introduction by Michael Gandy. Sessions Book Trust, c1998. Further volumes cover 'Other parts of North England including Isle of Man', 'Maryland,

*George Fox was imprisoned in Launceston Castle.*

New England and West Indies', 'London and Middlesex', 'Ireland, Scotland and Wales', 'South West England', 'Southern England' and 'East Anglia & East Midlands'.

The Meeting for Sufferings relied on reports from its county correspondents. Books of Sufferings were kept by both Monthly and Quarterly Meetings. These, together with the *Great Books*, enable us to trace the rise and fall of religious repression between the seventeenth and the nineteenth centuries. They can be compared with the evidence provided by the records of Quarter Sessions and church courts, so that both sides of the story can be seen. Quaker 'testimonies against tithes' are particularly voluminous, so much so that model testimonies were issued for the guidance of Friends. The records reveal the extent of financial suffering caused by such testimonies and include much information on imprisonment, fines and the seizure of goods. They also record many tithe disputes with clergy, tithe collectors, magistrates and others. A modern study of 'Sufferings' is provided by:

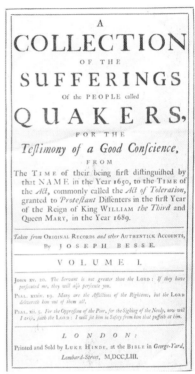

*Besse's* A Collection of Sufferings.

• Horle, Craig W. *The Quakers and the English Legal System, 1660-1688*. (University of Pennsylvania Press, 1988).

See also:

• Braithwaite, W.C. *The Penal Laws Affecting Early Friends in England*. (1907).
• Quaker Sufferings records: an 'embarras de richesse' **http://quakerstrongrooms.org/2012/06/06/quaker-sufferings-records-an-embarras-de-richesse**

## REGISTERS OF BIRTHS MARRIAGES AND BURIALS

Friends had an efficient system of registration. That was officially recognized in 1753, when Hardwicke's Marriage Act exempted Quakers from the requirement that all marriages (other than those of Jews) had to take place in the Church of England.

### Early Registration

Quaker registers began in the 1650s. They record births rather than baptisms, as Quakers did not baptise. Early Quakers sometimes recorded their own birth dates, so that some registers include entries dating back to the reign of Elizabeth I. Generally, Monthly Meetings took responsibility for compiling the registers, although occasionally – as at Leeds – local registers may also be found. Prior to 1776, when the London Yearly Meeting introduced a new system of registration, there was no uniformity in the entries made in registers. Frequently, birth entries merely give the name of the child and its parents, with the date of its birth. Where both parents were Friends, children had birth-right membership. If this was not the case and one parent was not a Friend, then there was no birth-right membership and the entry would be annotated 'NM', i.e. non-member. Sometimes, more information was given. In some registers, space was left under marriage entries for the names of children to be added.

Marriage certificates began to be issued in 1677, and were elaborate. They might include not only the names of the couple, but also the groom's occupation, the names and occupations of the parents of both parties, a detailed statement concerning the intention of the couple and the names of witnesses, who sometimes included everyone present. The marriage register often summarized all this information, but sometimes the certificate was copied verbatim, taking up a page or two of the register. On occasion, the certificate itself might be used to record the names of the couple's children and grandchildren.

Death entries in Quaker registers normally record the place of burial. In the early years, before Quakers had their own burial grounds, that sometimes took place in parish churchyards and was recorded in parish registers. Many preferred to be buried in their own orchards and fields; that too might be recorded in parish registers. By 1700, most Meetings had their own burial grounds and kept their own registers – although occasionally an entry might be duplicated in the parish register. Information about burial grounds is likely to be found in Monthly Meeting minutes and other records. Not all Quakers necessarily used them. Friends had little veneration for burial places and some continued the practice of burial on their own property. Monumental inscriptions were regarded as a 'vain custom' and discouraged until the mid-nineteenth century. Even those erected since have not always been well treated and some have disappeared. Quaker family historians will find few inscriptions to aid their researches.

### Post-1776 Registration

In 1776, Quaker registration procedures were reformed. The Quakers followed the example set by the Church of England under Hardwicke's Marriage Act of 1753 and began to use printed books to record registration details. Whereas Hardwicke's Act solely concerned marriages, the Quakers' forms covered births and deaths as well. Birth notes and death notes, which a few Meetings had introduced previously, were now standardized and used throughout the Society. Duplicate registers were kept by both Monthly Meetings and Quarterly Meetings. Preparative Meetings, if they wished, could also keep registers.

In order to register a birth, two birth notes were prepared by the Preparative Meeting and sent to the Monthly Meeting. After the details had been entered in the register, the registrar would sign both copies, hand one back to the parents and send the other to the Quarterly Meeting for re-registration. The details given included the names of the child and its parents, the place and date of birth and the names of three or four witnesses.

After 1776, marriage certificates had to be compiled in duplicate by the couple themselves and sent to the bride's Monthly Meetings, who copied them into their registers. One certificate was retained on file, the other was sent to the Quarterly Meeting for re-registration. If the couple belonged to different Monthly Meetings, a copy was sent to the husband's Meeting. From 1794, only abstracts of certificates were registered.

Burial notes were also completed in duplicate and registered by the Monthly Meeting who owned the burial ground. Notes frequently took the form of an instruction to the gravedigger to prepare a grave. He would be instructed to return the note so that the burial could be registered. A copy of the note was sent to the Quarterly Meeting for re-registration. If the deceased was a member of a different Monthly Meeting, they would also be sent a burial note for entry in their register. The entry in the register would include the name of the deceased, the date of death, age, residence, occupation and where buried. After 1776, Quaker registers provide far more information than the registers of other denominations.

### Finding Pre-1837 Registers

Most pre-1837 Quaker registers were surrendered to the Registrar General in 1840 and again in 1857. Surrendered registers (together with some birth and burial notes and marriage certificates) are in The National Archives, class RG 6,[5] and are listed in:

• *General Register Office. Society of Friends registers, notes and certificates of births, marriages and deaths.* (List & Index Society 267, 1996). This volume has a useful introduction to the registers. It supersedes previous listings, which should not now be used.

Registers held by The National Archives are now available on a pay-per-view internet database:

• BMD Registers
  **www.bmdregisters.co.uk**

Lists of Quaker registers held by both The National Archives and local record offices can also be found in the county volumes of the *National Index of Parish Registers*, published by the Society of Genealogists.

## Digests of Births, Marriages and Deaths

Before the pre-1837 registers were surrendered, digests were made of them. These digests are arranged geographically in Quarterly Meeting areas. They are not transcripts and are not arranged in the same order as the original registers. Rather, entries are made chronologically, in decennial periods, under each letter of the alphabet. Not all the information provided in the original registers is recorded in the digests. For example, witnesses are systematically excluded. Digests should be treated as indexes to the original registers, not the originals themselves.

The Digests were made in duplicate. One copy was kept by the Monthly Meeting and may now be in a local record office. The other copy is held by Friends House Library. A microfilm of the Friends House Library copy has been made and may be found in some libraries:

- *Quaker digest registers of births, marriages and burials for England and Wales, c.1650-1837.* 32 reels + pamphlet. World Microfilms Publications, 1989. These digests record some 260,000 births, 40,000 marriages and 310,000 deaths.

## Post-1837 Registration

On the introduction of civil registration in 1837, Quakers adapted their system. Each Monthly Meeting was required to appoint its own registration officer for marriages. The marriage register was to be compiled in duplicate in a printed book supplied by the Registrar General. These books were almost identical to those used by the Church of England and, after 1898, by other Nonconformist denominations (see above, p.66). On completion, one copy of the book was returned to the District Registrar, the other was retained by the Monthly Meeting (and may now frequently be found deposited in record offices). The Registrar had to make quarterly returns of marriages direct to the Registrar General. Friends continued to use a revised form of their own marriage certificate. These were similar to those used previously and were quite distinct from the marriage certificates that could be obtained from the General Register Office and District Registrars.

Monthly and Quarterly Meetings ceased to compile registers of births and deaths. However, the system of birth and death notices was continued in order to keep records of members. Receipt of these notices was minuted, the members' registers annotated and the note retained for the record. In 1860, a digest of events recorded since 1837 was begun. Meetings were asked to compile a digest of all events between 1837 and 1860 and, for the future, to send in annual return of births, deaths and marriages. That continued to be done until 1961, when the birth and death digests were closed. However, the marriage digest continues to be maintained.

### Supplementary Death Records

Some Meetings supplemented their death registers by keeping a record of wills in which Friends were names as executors. The registers are also supplemented by London Yearly Meeting 'testimonies concerning ministers deceased'. Friends House Library hold these testimonies from c.1717 to 1872. Since that date, they have been printed in the proceedings of London Yearly Meeting, together with testimonies relating to other Friends. The latter record the answers to queries sent to Quarterly and Yearly Meetings and are also recorded in the minutes of those Meetings, or perhaps in separate books amongst their archives.

### MEETING HOUSES

Meeting house licences (see above, pp.45–7) provide basic information about Quaker meeting houses, but much more may be learnt from the records of Monthly Meetings. The meeting house was the most important part of a Meeting's property. Trust deeds and other documents relating to the property of Meetings will identify trustees, who were generally chosen from amongst the more substantial Friends. Quaker meeting houses were normally built plainly and inexpensively. Utilitarianism and simplicity were demanded by Quaker beliefs. Unlike the chapels of other denominations, they were likely to be used for more purposes than just worship. School was frequently conducted in them during the week. Rural meeting houses were generally rustic constructions. In

*Inside Jordans Quaker Meeting House, Buckinghamshire.* (Courtesy Wikimedia).

towns they were often more imposing, but that was due to the fact that they had to accommodate more people.

For a detailed survey of Quaker meeting houses, with full descriptions of individual buildings, see:

• Butler, David M. *The Quaker meeting houses of Britain: an account of the some 1300 meeting houses and 900 burial grounds in England, Wales and Scotland, from the start of the movement in 1652 to the present time and research guide to sources.* (2 vols. Friends Historical Society, 1999).

Briefer accounts are provided by:

• Lidbetter, Hubert. *The Friends Meeting House: an historical survey of the places of worship of the Society of Friends (Quakers) from the*

*days of their founder, George Fox, in the 17th century, to the present day.* (2nd ed. Ebor Press, 1979).
- Southall, Kenneth H. *Our Quaker Heritage: early meeting houses built prior to 1720 and in use today: photographs and word pictures from the past.* (2nd ed. Quaker Home Service, 1984).

See also:

- Butler, David M. 'Meeting Houses built and Meetings settled: answers to the Yearly Meeting queries, 1688-1791', *Journal of the Friends Historical Society* 51, 1965–7, pp.174–211.

For Quaker meeting houses and other property in Devon, consult:

- Dymond, Francis W. *Trust Property within the County of Devon.* (Devon and Cornwall Quarterly Meeting, 1899).

## FINANCE

Every Meeting, at every level in the Society, had its own 'stock' of money to supply its needs and therefore kept its own accounts. Account books and subscription lists frequently survive. They provide valuable information on Society income and expenditure. It may be possible to identify who gave what and thus to assess the relative prosperity of Friends. It may also be possible to identify 'sufferers' and other recipients of relief. The accounts are likely to reveal how funds were dispersed and provide an indication of the matters which Friends felt to be important. Funds were collected in Particular Meetings, but collection was supervised by Monthly Meetings, who took a keen interest in raising money for the national stock. Legacies were also an important source of finance and the minutes and accounts of trust funds may provide useful information to researchers. Expenditure might cover the maintainance of meeting houses and burial grounds, charitable giving (including relief for Quaker poor), education, apprenticeship, and the legal costs of Friends who suffered persecution.

## QUAKER POOR RELIEF

Friends ran an effective system of poor relief for their own members, who were frequently denied relief by parish overseers. They were determined to provide both financial and moral support to members who suffered persecution for their beliefs. They also supported members who experienced fire, flood, and other accidents. The financial support they provided was similar to that provided by the officers of the Poor Law, even to the establishment of a system of 'settlement' determining eligibility for relief from specific Monthly Meetings. From 1710, Friends who moved into a new area were required to obtain a 'settlement certificate' to present to their new Monthly Meeting. There were elaborate rules for establishing who was 'settled' in the area of a specific Monthly Meeting and thus eligible for relief from that Meeting. These rules were abolished in 1861.

Quakers also attached great importance to ensuring that young people, especially the poor, were apprenticed, so that they could become self-reliant. Monthly Meeting minutes regularly record payments for placing apprentices.

Much pastoral work was undertaken by Women's Meetings. Their minutes often provide information about the recipients of relief. Further information can be found in the detailed correspondence between Meetings about the relief of particular individuals.

Valuable information about the poor and social action can be gleaned from Quaker records of poor relief. As an example of what can be discovered, see:

• Prichard, Muriel F. Lloyd. 'Norfolk Friends care of their poor', *Journal of the Friends Historical Society* 39, 1947, pp.18–32; 40, 1948, pp.3–18.

The Quaker Workhouse at Clerkenwell is the subject of:

• Hitchcock, Timothy V., ed. *Richard Hutton's Complaints Book: the Notebook of the Steward of the Quaker Workhouse at Clerkenwell, 1711-1737.* (London Record Society, 24, 1987). Digitized at **www.british-history.ac.uk/london-record-soc/vol24/vii-xxiii**

## QUAKER EDUCATION

The Quakers were active in education, both as a Society and as private individuals. At the local level, they frequently made their premises available for schools. Monthly Meeting minutes may record arrangements for teachers to be paid by fees or bequests. Many meeting houses had libraries, which can also be traced in the minutes.

A number of boarding schools were established by Committees of the Society in the eighteenth and especially the nineteenth centuries; these included, for example, Sidcot and Ackworth. There were also a number of private schools run by Friends. Admission registers frequently survive. Some have been printed. Friends House Library has indexes to a number of others. Annual reports, school magazines and other records may also be available.

A bibliography and guide to the records of Quaker schools is provided by:

• 'Quaker schools in Great Britain and Ireland: a selective bibliography and guide to records', *Quaker Connections* 29, 2003, pp.10–17. There is an internet version of this bibliography (revised in 2009) at **www.quaker.org.uk./resources/library/ about-the-collections** (scroll down and click 'schools').

A number of articles in *Quaker Connections* (see below, p.148) list the archives of Quaker schools. See, for example:

• Morris, Bridget. 'The archives of Bootham School, York', *Quaker Connections* 30, 2003, pp.20–2.

## QUAKER BIOGRAPHICAL DICTIONARIES

Much information about Friends can be found in biographical dictionaries. The best published work is now:

• Milligan, Edward H. *Biographical Dictionary of British Quakers in Commerce and Industry, 1775-1920*. (Sessions Book Trust, 2007). This includes a useful glossary and bibliography.

Milligan draws heavily on a typescript work, the *Dictionary of Quaker Biography*, which is available at Friends House Library and also at Haverford College Library in the USA. It includes biographies of c.20,000 Friends. A digital version is currently in preparation; see:

- Digital Dictionary of Quaker Biography
  **trilogy.brynmawr.edu/speccoll/dictionary**

For an older work, see:

- *Biographical catalogue, being an account of the lives of Friends and others whose portraits are in the London Friends Institute . . .* (Friends Institute, 1888).

Much biographical information on leading Friends can be found by consulting their journals. Many 'travelling Friends' kept them and they contain valuable information, not only on their authors, but also on the Quaker history of the places they visited. See:

- Winchester, Angus. 'Travellers in grey: Quaker journals as a source for local history', *Local Historian* 21(2), 1991, pp.70–5.

For a published journal, see:

- Jones, Hannah, ed. *The Life & Times of a Charlbury Quaker: the Journals of William Jones 1784-1818*. (Oxfordshire Record Society 69, 2014).

## QUAKER PERIODICALS
Quakers, like other Nonconformists, could subscribe to a number of denominational publications. The *Friend* (1843– ) and the *British Friend* (1843–1913), were commenced almost simultaneously. Both carried notices of births, marriages and deaths (birth notices in the *Friend* from 1850). From 1894, the *Friend* carried obituaries; an index to them is held by Friends House Library. Other journals are listed by Altholz (see above, p.56).

The official *An account of the times of holding the quarterly, monthly and preparative meetings, and of the meetings for worship of the Society of Friends in England, Wales and Scotland* (also known as the *Book of Meetings . . .*) has been published annually since 1789 and gives details of local meetings.

The Society of Friends also published *The Annual Monitor and Memorandum Book (or, Obituary of the members of the Society of Friends)* between 1813 and 1919/20. Its obituaries (prior to 1892) are indexed in:

• Green, J.J. *Quaker records: being an index to 'The Annual monitor', 1813-1892, containing over twenty thousand obituary notices of members of the Society of Friends*. (Edward Hicks, 1894).

## THE QUAKER CALENDAR

Quakers used the normal calendar, except that they refused to use the pagan names of days and months. Sunday therefore became the 'first day', Tuesday the 'second day', and so on. The months were a little more complicated. Until 1752, September, October, November and December could be used, since these merely translated numbers and were numerically correct since the year began on 25 March. The alteration of the calendar in 1752, so that the year began on 1 January, meant that none of these names of months could truthfully be used, so January (which had been the eleventh month) became the first month, February the second and so on. It is advisable, when recording information from Quaker records pre-1752, to copy the date as it is given and to add the new-style date in brackets. More detail is provided by a Friends House Library leaflet on:

• The Quaker Calendar
  **www.quaker.org.uk**
  (on the 'about the collections' section of the Library page)

## FURTHER READING

Quakers left an extensive paper trail that is ripe for research. They were mindful of the needs of future historians: George Fox himself made detailed provisions for the preservation of his manuscripts. The handbooks listed above, pp.74–5, and especially the work by Steel, include much useful information on Quaker records. A guide solely devoted to Quakers is offered by:

- Milligan, Edward H., & Thomas, Malcolm J. *My Ancestors were Quakers: how can I find out more about them?* (2nd ed. Society of Genealogists, 1999).

See also:

- Mortimer, R.S. 'The archives of the Society of Friends (Quakers)', *Amateur Historian* 3, 1956–8, pp.55–61.
- Utah Valley Regional Family History Center Brigham Young University Harold B. Lee Library: Research Guide: Religious Society Of Friends (Quakers) Genealogical & Historical Records **http://files.lib.byu.edu/family-history-library/research-outlines/NonGeographic/Quaker.pdf**

For information on Quaker research in Yorkshire, see:

- Roberts, Helen. 'Coming up out of the North: the Yorkshire Quaker Heritage Project', *Local Historian* 30(4), 2000, pp.260–4.
- Yorkshire Quaker History Project **www.hull.ac.uk/oldlib/archives/quaker/index.htm** This includes a research guide, a database, lists of Meeting Houses and Meetings and a variety of other useful pages. The research guide is also available in print:
- Roberts, Helen E. *Researching Yorkshire Quaker history: a guide to sources*. (University of Hull Brynmor Jones Library, 2003).

A useful bibliography of publications relating to Friends is:

- Smith, Joseph. *A descriptive catalogue of Friends books, or, books written by members of the Society of Friends, commonly called Quakers, from their first rise to the present time, interspersed with critical remarks and occasional biographical notices.* (2 vols + supplement. Joseph Smith, 1867–93).

Friends House Library possess an extensive library of Quaker literature. Holdings include not just books and pamphlets, but also many periodicals, illustrations, the archives of a variety of Quaker organizations and a number of personal collections of manuscripts, such as those of Margaret Fell, Elizabeth Fry and the Gurney family. The latter are listed in:

• Eddington, Arthur J. *Synopsis of the Gurney manuscripts deposited in the library of the Religious Society of Friends.* (List & Index Society special series 8, 1973).

The Library's webpage includes guides to 'genealogical sources', 'Quakers and World War I', 'Quaker Schools in Great Britain and Ireland, 'Conscientious Objectors and the Peace Movement in Britain 1914–1945', as well as a number of others. These can be found by clicking the relevant buttons at:

• The Religious Society of Friends in Britain: Library: About the Collections **www.quaker.org.uk/resources/library/about-the-collections**

See also:

• 'Genealogical sources in Friends House Library', *Quaker Connections* 6, 1995, pp.21–3.
• Hicks, Muriel A. 'Manuscript resources of the Friends libraries: the Library, Friends House, London', in Brinton, Anna Cox, ed. *Then and Now: Quaker essays, historical and contemporary.* (University of Pennsylvania Press, 1960).

Quaker historians should also investigate the records of the established church, which record their persecution from the persecutors' point of view. Some of these have already been discussed in Chapter 2. See also:

*Swarthmore Hall, home of Margaret Fell and base of the early Quakers.*

- Barber, Melanie. 'Records of Quaker interest in Lambeth Palace Library', *Journal of the Friends Historical Society* 53, 1972–5, pp.165–9.

The archives of Quarterly and Monthly Meetings have usually been deposited in local record offices and other repositories. Some are listed on the webpage of the Quaker Family History Society (see below). They can also be traced by using the web-based union catalogues listed above, pp.28–9. A particularly useful catalogue of 'The records of the Society of Friends in Norfolk' has been produced by Norfolk Record Office and is available by searching The National Archives Discovery catalogue **discovery.nationalarchives.gov.uk**. It includes a detailed guide to Quaker records.

Family historians should join the Quaker Family History Society, whose website includes introductions to various types of records, together with county pages showing what records are available locally:

- Quaker Family History Society
  **www.rootsweb.ancestry.com/~engqfhs**

The Society also regularly publishes *Quaker Connections* (1994– ), which should be checked by all researchers. Another important periodical is the *Journal of the Friends' Historical Society*. See:

- The Friends Historical Society
  **http://f-h-s.org.uk**

Leeds University houses two collections of Quaker archives from Yorkshire and has a database of Meeting minute books from the West and North Ridings:

- Quaker Collections Guide
  **http://library.leeds.ac.uk/special-collections-quaker**

The essential handbook for students of Quakerism is:

- Angell, Stephen W., & Dandelion, Pink. *The Oxford Handbook of Quaker Studies*. Oxford Handbooks in religion and theology. (Oxford University Press, 2013).

Useful general histories of Quakers include:

- Braithwaite, William C. *The Beginnings of Quakerism*. (2nd ed. Oxford University Press, 1912).
- Braithwaite, William C. *The Second Period of Quakerism*. (2nd ed. William Sessions, 1979).
- Jones, Rufus M. *The Later Periods of Quakerism*. (2 vols. Macmillan and Co., 1921).
- Davies, Adrian. *The Quakers in English Society 1655-1725*. (Clarendon Press, 2000).
- Isichei, Elizabeth Allo. *Victorian Quakers*. (Oxford University Press, 1970).
- Kennedy, T.C. *British Quakerism: 1860-1920: the transformation of a religious community*. (Oxford University Press, 2001).
- Lloyd, Arnold. *Quaker Social History, 1669-1738*. (Longmans, Green, 1950).
- Moore, R. *The Light in their Consciences: the Early Quakers in Britain, 1644-1666*. (Pennsylvania State University Press, 2000).
- Reay, Barry. *The Quakers and the English Revolution*. (Temple-Smith, 1985).
- Vann, Richard T. *The Social Development of English Quakerism, 1655-1755*. (Harvard University Press, 1969).

For examples of good local studies, see:

- Scott, David. *Quakerism in York 1650-1780*. Borthwick paper 80. (Borthwick Institute, 1981).
- Morgan, Nicholas. *Lancashire Quakers and the establishment, 1660-1730*. (Ryburn Academic, 1993).
- Wright, Sheila. *Friends in York: the dynamics of Quaker revival 1780-1860*. (Keele University Press, 1995).

A number of works offer excerpts from early sources:

- Barbour, Hugh, & Roberts, Arthur O., eds. *Early Quaker Writings, 1650-1700*. (William B. Eerdmans, 1973).

- *Extracts from state papers relating to Friends. First series, 1654 to 1672. Journal* supplement 8–9. (Friends Historical Society, 1910–13).
- Penney, Norman, ed. *The first publishers of truth: being early records (now first printed) of the introduction of Quakerism into the counties of England and Wales.* (Headley, 1907).

A variety of early Quaker sources are also available online at:

- A Quaker Page
  **www.strecorsoc.org/quaker.html**

The important Swarthmore papers, held by the library of the Society of Friends, have been microfilmed and are available in some libraries as:

- *The Quaker manuscript collection.* (15 reels. World Microfilm Publications, 1979–80).

Finally, some food for thought for Quaker historians is provided by:

- Punshon, John. 'The significance of the tradition: reflections on the writing of Quaker history', *Journal of the Friends Historical Society* 60(2), 2005, pp.77–96.

# Chapter 5

# THE METHODISTS

By the beginning of the eighteenth century, the old Dissent had settled down into the groove it had carved out for itself in British society, and had ceased to be concerned with evangelism. And the Church of England breathed a sigh of relief. It could not destroy Dissent – but it could contain it. Nonconformity had ceased to pose a serious threat to the established order.

Churchmen were unaware, however, that 'enthusiasm' was about to break out in their midst, indeed, in their heartland. Most clergy were educated at either Oxford or Cambridge. It was at Oxford that George Whitefield experienced conversion in 1735 and joined with the Wesley brothers to form the derisively named 'Holy Club'. Their contemporaries called them Methodists, because they sought to live their Christian lives methodically.

It was not the intention of these clergymen of the Church of England to form a new denomination. Rather, they sought revival within the established church, and Charles Wesley in particular resisted any thought of creating a separate denomination throughout his life. The Wesleys did, however, undertake extensive missionary journeys throughout the UK. In doing so, they founded many societies and classes, from which, eventually, various Methodist denominations grew. Whilst the Wesleys were alive, society members attended their own sermons and prayer meetings, but they were also punctilious about attending their parish churches.

Methodist 'enthusiasm' was a 'horrid thing' in the view of some bishops, perhaps especially in view of the social classes associated with it. Methodists tended to be drawn from the ranks of skilled tradesmen and the lower middle classes; few were poor, but, equally,

*The Holy Club in session.*

few were gentlemen. The bishops refused to have anything to do with the movement and would not ordain Methodist clergy. The Methodist societies could not sustain themselves without ordained clergy, but they could not remain within the Church of England whilst conducting their own ordinations. John Wesley found himself compelled – much to his brother's horror – to claim the right to ordain priests himself. Wesleyan Methodism ceased being an association of the devout within the Church of England and became a denomination in its own right.

The first Methodist conference was held in 1744, long before the first clergy were ordained. John Wesley called a meeting of his fellow preachers, in order to obtain their collective advice. The Conference resolved to meet annually, and still does. Until Wesley's death, its sole role was to advise him, nothing more. Wesley reserved decision-making powers to himself whilst he lived. His 1784 'Deed of Declaration' made provision for 100 senior preachers – the 'legal hundred' – to assume responsibility for the many Methodist societies he had founded after his death.[1] No provision was made for lay representation – a fact which led to demands for greater democracy and to a number of breakaway movements. It was not until 1877 that Conference admitted lay representatives.

The structure of the embryo denomination was established at the 1744 Conference. Each congregation became a 'society' which belonged to a 'circuit', to which preachers were appointed. Each circuit had ten or fifteen societies, which built their own chapels. Circuits joined together into 'districts', which could keep an eye on Methodist activities over a wide area.

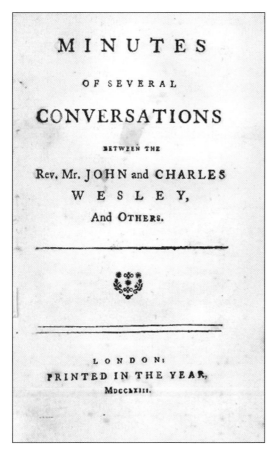

*The first printed minutes of a Methodist Conference, 1749.*

Wesleyan Methodism was united until the death of the Wesleys – although it should be borne in mind that the Wesleys were not the only members of the Holy Club to found new denominations (see Chapter 6). The Wesley brothers held their societies together by sheer force of character. After their deaths, Wesleyan Methodism continued to be united in its doctrine, but failed in its attempt to maintain denominational unity. The ministerial control which John Wesley had imposed was challenged by those who wanted more lay involvement and more democratic governance. In 1797, Alexander Kilham led the Methodist New Connexion in the first schism. In the north, the Primitive Methodists broke away in 1807. On the borders of Devon and Cornwall, the Bible Christians founded their own denomination

*Wesleyan Chapel, Penzance.*

in 1815. The Tent Methodists broke away in 1820, although they only survived until 1832. Protestant Methodists were formed in Leeds in 1827 and the Wesleyan Methodist Association began in 1836.

Wesley himself was a Tory, but some of the groups which broke away from his conference were more radical. Many, and perhaps especially the Primitive Methodists, were involved in radical politics and trade unionism, seeing such activity as a part of their Christian witness, and deriving their campaigning techniques from their experience as local preachers and class leaders. Joseph Arch, for example, was the Primitive Methodist local preacher who founded the National Agricultural Labourers' Union, and subsequently became a Member of Parliament. The records of trade unionism may be worth exploring for evidence relating to Methodism. A number of introductions to these records are available:

• Crail, Mark. *Tracing your Labour Movement Ancestors: a guide for family historians.* (Pen & Sword, 2009).
• Southall, Humphrey, Gilbert, David, & Bryce, Carol. *Nineteenth Century Trade Union Records: an Introduction and Select Guide.* Historical Geography Research Series 27. (Historical Geography Research Group, 1994).
• Trade Union Ancestors
**www.unionancestors.co.uk**

In 1857, the Protestant Methodists and the Wesleyan Methodist Association came together with reformers from the Wesleyan Methodists and formed the United Methodist Free Church. Other reformers founded the Wesleyan Reform Union at the same time. Fifty years later, three denominations – the United Methodists, the Methodist New Connexion and the Bible Christians – came together to form the United Methodist Church. In 1932, the Methodist Church was formed by a union of the Wesleyan Methodists, the Primitive Methodists and the United Methodists. The Wesleyan Reform Union **www.thewru.com** and a few independent Methodist churches, are also still in existence. For a list of independent Methodist societies, see:

- 'Independent Methodist societies: a checklist', *Proceedings of the Wesley Historical Society* 33, 1961–2, pp.5–10.

A number of other denominations also have Methodist connections, but will be dealt with in Chapters 6 and 8.

## CONNEXIONAL ARCHIVES

Those denominations which sprang from Wesleyan Methodism all had the same basic organizational structure – Conference, the Districts, the Circuits and the Societies. It was within this structure that the records of Methodism were created. The records of Conference, and of many central organizations, are now held by the John Rylands University Library of Manchester, in its Methodist Archives and Research Centre (MARC) (see below, pp.174–5). Early records of the Wesleyan Methodist Conference show that its attention was primarily focused on the preaching ministry. It also reviewed Methodism's numerical and financial strength and sought to identify fresh opportunities for conducting the work of the Gospel. These issues have continued to be of prime concern, but a wide range of other topics also increasingly demanded attention. Today, Conference has to hear and respond to the reports of numerous committees and has to determine Methodist policy on a much broader range of topics than it faced in the eighteenth century.

The Journal is the definitive record of Conference. It contains much sensitive information, and is closed to researchers for 75 years. The published minutes record the decisions of Conference, but do not include much information on its detailed discussions. Their content has varied in the past, but lists of attendees, preachers' stations for the coming year, and obituaries of preachers have all been included since the eighteenth century. More recently, minutes have included lists of preachers' names and addresses and much financial information. Researchers may also find it useful to consult Conference agendas, which Wesleyan Methodists have had printed since 1881. For a useful guide to eighteenth and nineteenth century Conference records, see:

• Swift, Wesley F. 'The minutes of Conference', *Proceedings of the Wesley Historical Society* 31, 1957–8, pp.155–60.

A detailed index to the minutes is provided by:

• Wansbrough, Charles E. *Handbook and index to the minutes of the Conference, showing the growth and development of the Wesleyan Methodist constitution from the first Conference, 1744, to 1890.* (Wesleyan Methodist Book Room, 1890).

A number of minutes have been digitized; for links to these, visit:

• Methodist Heritage: Online books: Minutes of Conference **www.methodistheritage.org.uk/research-online-books-minutes-of-conference.htm**

A variety of other records were created by the Wesleyan Conference, its committees and its departments. These covered topics as diverse as Home Missions, the Worn Out Ministers and Widows Fund and Sunday schools. MARC also holds the Conference records of the other Methodist denominations which united in 1907 and 1933. Many records are available for the Primitive Methodists, but unfortunately other denominations are less well documented. A detailed guide to the Connexional archives is provided by:

• Guide to the Conference Collection **www.library.manchester.ac.uk/search-resources/guide-to-special-collections/methodist/using-the-collections/guide-to -the-conference-collection/**

### Methodist Districts
Districts group together a number of circuits in order to oversee Methodist activities at the regional level and to ensure that decisions of Conference are implemented. The early minutes of their half-yearly meetings recorded their deliberations in question and answer format, for example, 'Do we all believe and teach the old Methodist

doctrine?' Much attention was given to the preaching ministry and to doctrinal questions. The building of new chapels was encouraged, boys were sent to Kingswood and other Methodist schools and collections for particular projects were organized. The minutes and other records of Methodist Districts, can usually be found in MARC, but some have been deposited in county record offices.

**Methodist Circuits**
The circuit is the basis of local Methodist administration. Conference appoints ministers to circuits, not to individual chapels. Each circuit normally includes a number of societies and in the countryside may cover a wide area, with some chapels being 20 or 30 miles from others in the same circuit. The changing boundaries of circuits may cause problems, as particular societies may have been included in several different circuits in the course of their history. It should also be noted that the boundaries of circuits sometimes ignored county boundaries. Researchers need to be aware of boundaries when searching for the records of a particular society.

Circuits were governed by their Quarterly Meetings, the minutes of which record their deliberations and identify attendees. Much of their business was concerned with finance and property. Accounts record income and expenditure – the latter frequently exceeding the former in the nineteenth century. Property schedules and trust deeds (see below, p.164) record the property circuits owned, and lists of trustees give the names of those responsible for administering it. Manses were usually the property of circuits rather than societies and both circuits and societies had some responsibility for chapels.

Other circuit records may include registers of members, class books, removal registers, the accounts of horse hire and other funds and a variety of other documents. For an example of circuit records in print, see:

• Costen, Michael David, ed. *Wesleyans and Bible Christians in South Somerset: accounts and minutes, 1808-1907.* (Somerset Record Society 78, 1984).

Accounts and a circuit plan from the late eighteenth century are printed in:

* 'Early Records at St. Just', *Proceedings of the Wesley Historical Society* 18(4), 1931, pp.71–5.

For circuit funding, see:

* Mills, F.H. 'Circuit Finance in Early Methodism', *Proceedings of the Wesley Historical Society* 23(3), 1941, pp.59–64; 23(4), 1941, pp.77–81; 23(5), 1942, pp.108–11; 23(6), 1942, pp.139–41.

Another interesting record (although whether it was strictly speaking a circuit record is debatable) is provided by:

* 'A Methodist sermon register of the eighteenth century', *Proceedings of the Wesley Historical Society* 9, 1914, pp.35–8 & 191–4.

Circuit and society records which are not in use have usually been deposited in local record offices. They are not normally to be found in MARC.

**Local Preachers and Circuit Plans**
One of the prominent features of Methodism was – and is – the local preacher. Every Methodist minister began his career as a local preacher. The origins of Methodist preachers are discussed in:

* Lenton, John H. *John Wesley's Preachers: a social and statistical analysis of the British and Irish preachers who entered the Methodist Itinerancy before 1791.* (Paternoster, 2009). Includes a list of preachers.

See also:

* Lenton, John. 'John Wesley and the travelling preachers', *Bulletin of the John Rylands University Library of Manchester* 85(2 & 3), 2003, pp.99–110.

Local preachers' meetings were held regularly in each circuit. Their minutes record much information about the men and women who offered themselves in this ministry and the rigorous selection and training programme they had to follow before becoming accredited. Local preachers' names may also be found on circuit plans, which set out the preaching programme for each quarter (or other period) and show who is scheduled to preach in each chapel. Circuit plans survive in profusion, not just amongst Circuit archives, but also in MARC, in other Methodist repositories and elsewhere. Indeed, the Society of Cirplanologists is devoted to their study, and publishes its journal, *Cirplan*, regularly. It has also published:

• Rose, Edward Alan. *A register of Methodist circuit plans*. (Society of Cirplanologists, 1965, + 5 supplements to 1980).

See also:

• Leary, William. *Methodist Preaching Plans: a guide to their usefulness to the historian*. (William Leary, 1977).
• Rose, E.A. 'The evolution of the Circuit Plan', *Proceedings of the Wesley Historical Society* 37, 1969–70, pp.50–4.

A good discussion of circuit plans, focusing on the Isle of Man, but of wider interest, is provided by:

• Circuit Plans
  **www.isle-of-man.com**/manxnotebook/methdism/plans.htm

**Methodist Society Records**
The society, with its chapel, was the basic unit of Methodist organization. Its 'Leaders Meeting' was responsible for the running of chapel affairs and its minutes are one of the major resources for chapel history. Minutes of annual meetings contain reports from committees and other organizations. Trustees were responsible for the maintenance of buildings and kept their own minutes. Much of the surviving documentation focuses on buildings and finance. The

# HULL CIRCUIT.

### Preachers Sunday Plan of the People called Primitive Methodists, known also by the Name of Ranters.

Pray ye therefore the Lord of the Harvest, that he will send forth Labourers into his Harvest.—Matt. ix. 38.

| 1819. Places and Time of Preaching. | AUG 1 | 8 | 15 | 22 | 29 | SEP 5 | 12 | 19 | 26 | OCT 3 | 10 | 17 | 24 | 31 |
|---|---|---|---|---|---|---|---|---|---|---|---|---|---|---|
| Mill-Street, 10½ and 6 | | | | | | | | i | 3 | 3 | 1 | i | 2 | 2 |
| Mill-Street, 3 | | | | | t | | | 8 | 5 | 4 | 7 | 11 | 10 | 9 |
| Penitentiary, 3 | 1 | 1 | T1 | T3 | T2 | L2 | 1 | 9 | 3 | 6 | 1 | 10 | 2 | 15 |
| Pottery, 3 | 10 | 5 | 6 | 11 | 7 | | 4 | 1 | 15 | 3 | 9 | 1 | 5 | 2 |
| Groves, 3 | 9 | | | 15 | | 9 | | 4 | | W.11 | 10 | | 6 | 4 |
| Hessle, 6 | 7 | 10 | 9 | T11 | 6 | 4 | 11 | 15 | 9 | 10 | 4 | 5 | 7 | 11B |
| Swanland, 6 | 5 | | 10 | T | 14 | | 6 | L7 | | | 15 | | 4 | |
| Woodmansey, 10—Cherry Burton, 2 | | 7 | | 12 | | 5 | | 10 | | 15 | | 13 | | 6 |
| Barrow, &c. | 2 | | L3T | | 10 | | | | 4 | | 5 | 9 | | |
| Elloughton, 10 | 15 | 13 | 12 | T4 | BD | 11 | 10 | 14 | 6 | 5 | 13 | 7 | 8 | 10 |
| Brantingham, 2 | 15 | | 12 | T | BD | | 10 | 6 | | | J.B | | 8 | |
| South-Cave, 10—Newbald, 2—North-Cave, 6 | | 2 | | L1T | | 3 | 2 | | | 1 | 2 | | | 3 |
| River-Bridge, 10 | * | 8 | T | 12 | | 14 | | 8 | | | 12 | 11 | | |
| North-Cave, 2 | * | | | 12 | | | | 8 | | | | 11 | | |
| South-Cave, 2 | | 11 | | | | | 8 | | | | 12 | | | |
| Newbald, 6 | * | 8 | 5 | 3 | | 8 | | 11 | | 8 | | 12 | | |
| Market-Weighton, 2 | | L5 | T | C3 54 | | 13 | | 11 | | 8 | | 12 | | |
| West-Cottinwith, 10—Weldrake, 2—Elvington, 6½ | 3 | 2 | | T1 | | 3 | | 2 | | 3 | 1 | | | |
| Ferrybridge, &c. | | 3 | 2 | | | T1 | | 3 | | 2 | | 3 | | 1 |

Names of Preachers.

1 W. CLOWES.
2 J. HARRISON.
3 S. HARRISON.
4 H. WOOLHOUSE.
5 J. WOOLHOUSE.
6 J. OXTOBY.
7 E. TAYLOR.
8 S. LAISTER.

ON TRIAL.

9 R. WOOLHOUSE.
10 W. RICKATESON.
11 J. COATS.
12 J. HEWSON.
13 E. VAUSE.
14 T. JOHNSON.
15 J. TAYLOR.

T. Tickets.—L. Lovefeast. C. Camp Meeting.

N. B. Quarter Day at Hull Sept. 13.—Local Preacher's Meeting to commence at Ten o'clock in the Morning.

☞ It is particularly requested that every Preacher will strictly attend his appointments; and in any place where he cannot attend, that he will provide a proper substitute.

JOHN HUTCHINSON, PRINTER, SILVER-STREET, HULL.

*A Primitive Methodist circuit plan..*

minutes of building sub-committees, for example, show how chapels came into existence. The accounts of society stewards can sometimes provide detailed information on income and expenditure. Pew rents in the early period were a major component of a society's income and are frequently separately recorded.[2] These records may provide useful sociological information, since seating arrangements reflected social standing. The names of members are recorded in church directories and community rolls and also in class books. The latter record the attendees of the weekly classes for bible study and prayer which were one of the major features of early Methodist activities. For class tickets, see:

- Beckerlegge, Oliver A. 'Non-Wesleyan class tickets', *Proceedings of the Wesley Historical Society* 32, 1959–60, pp.34–7, 48–51 & 88–90.
- Parkinson, F.M. 'Methodist class tickets', *Proceedings of the Wesley Historical Society* 1, 1898, pp.129–37.
- Verney, John. 'Early Wesleyan class tickets', *Proceedings of the Wesley Historical Society* 31, 1957–8, pp.2–9, 34–8 & 70–3.
- Wright, Joseph G. 'Class and band tickets: a guide to collectors', *Proceedings of the Wesley Historical Society* 5, 1906, pp.33–44.

Similarly, the names of children who attended Sunday Schools were sometimes recorded. A variety of other records may also be available, for example, the minutes and accounts of the Band of Hope, the Wesley Guild, Christian Endeavour, youth clubs and ladies' meetings.

## METHODIST BAPTISM, MARRIAGE AND BURIAL REGISTERS

Methodists regarded themselves as devout Anglicans until after John Wesley's death in 1791. Therefore, most Methodist baptisms, marriages and burials prior to this date were recorded in Church of England parish registers. Very few Methodist registers commence earlier than this. It was not until 1812 that Conference stressed the need to maintain baptismal registers. Nineteenth-century registers were sometimes maintained by circuits, sometimes by societies and sometimes both.

Most Methodist registers are baptismal registers. They frequently record dates of birth and mothers' maiden names. Few death registers survive, except where the Methodists had their own burial grounds. That is despite the fact that Methodist Conference in 1803 ordered that death registers be kept by each circuit.

Prior to 1838, the law required Methodists to marry in their parish churches. The introduction of civil registration in that year allowed them to marry in their own chapels, but only in the presence of a district registrar. It was rare for Methodists to maintain a separate register of marriages before 1898, when Methodist 'authorized persons' were given authority to record marriages in their own chapels. Since that date, Methodist marriage registers have conformed to the pattern described above, p.66.

Many Methodist registers were surrendered to the Registrar General in 1837 and again in 1857. These are now in The National Archives, in classes RG 4 and RG 8. In addition to the list mentioned above (pp.67–8), they are also listed by Leary (see below, p.180) and can be identified on the Discovery catalogue **http://discovery. nationalarchives.gov.uk**. These registers are now available online on the pay per view BMD Registers website **www.bmdregisters. co.uk**.

Those registers which were not surrendered, together with post-1837 baptism registers, post-1898 marriage registers and occasional burial registers, may be found in local record offices, or sometimes in Circuit safes. Copies of surrendered registers may also occasionally be found. Those in local record offices are sometimes included in the Discovery catalogue. All surviving registers should be listed in the county volumes of the Society of Genealogists' *National Index of Parish Registers*.

## THE WESLEYAN METROPOLITAN REGISTRY
In 1818, the Wesleyan Methodists began the Wesleyan Metropolitan Registry for the registration of births and baptisms. This continued until the advent of civil registration, and over 10,000 entries were made in the registers. Ministers made duplicate returns to the Registry on printed forms signed by parents and witnesses. When the details from these returns had been entered in the register, one copy was filed, the other was returned to the parents with a certificate stating the date of registration and noting the volume and folio numbers of the entry. These registers, with the filed certificates, were surrendered to the Registrar General and are now in The National Archives, class RG5. They are available on the BMD Registers database **www.bmdregisters.co.uk**.

## METHODIST CHAPELS
The earliest Methodist chapel was the New Room at Bristol, opened in 1739. It was not, however, until the nineteenth century that Methodist chapel-building began in earnest. The progress of chapel-building can be traced in trust deeds and other circuit records, in the

correspondence and diaries of ministers and laymen and in various other records. Circuit and district minutes recorded the progress of fund-raising and building. Methodist journals reported the opening of new chapels. Connexional archives, and particularly the records of the Connexional Property Division, may also contain much information on matters such as fund-raising, capacity, the names of trustees, and redundancy. MARC also holds a register of enrolled Wesleyan chapel deeds, together with the extensive archive of the Chapel Committee (more recently, the Property Division). The latter include 696 folders documenting chapels circuit by circuit. The presence of chapels can also be traced in trade directories (see above, pp.56–7). Useful guidance on researching chapels is provided by:

- Researching the History of a Chapel
  **www.library.manchester.ac.uk/search-resources/guide-to-special-collections/methodist/using-the-collections/researching-the-history-of-a-chapel**

For the history of the Methodist model deed, see:

- Perkins, E. Benson. *Methodist Preaching Houses and the Laws: the story of the Model Deed*. (Epworth Press, 1952).

The task of locating Methodist trust deeds is discussed by:

- Dunstan, N.J. 'Methodist enrolled deeds at the Public Record Office', *Proceedings of the Wesley Historical Society* 37, 1969–70, pp.151–3. See also 46, 1979–80, pp.19–24 & 34.

The earliest mention of Methodist connections with a particular place is likely to be identified in:

- *An Itinerary in which are traced the Rev John Wesley's journeys from October 14, 1735, to October 24, 1790*. (Supplement to Proceedings of the Wesley Historical Society 6, 1908). Available online at **www.biblicalstudies.org.uk/pdf/whs/06-supp.pdf**.

*Amesbury Methodist Church.*

See also:

- Register of Charles Wesley's Preaching
  https://divinity.duke.edu/initiatives-centers/cswt/research-resources/cw-register

*Bethania Wesleyan Chapel, Penmachno.*

Many Methodist buildings are included in the inventories of Nonconformist chapels compiled by Stell (see above, p.58). For a model county handlist of Methodist chapels, see:

• Thorne, Roger F.S. *Methodism in Devon: a handlist of chapels and their records*. (2nd ed. Devon Record Office, 1989).

## METHODIST MINISTERS AND LAYMEN

Records relating to local preachers have already been discussed. Every Methodist minister began his career as a local preacher, so these records should be consulted if information is being sought on a particular minister. Ministers, as already noted, were appointed to particular circuits. A number of works list circuits and ministers. The John Rylands Library page on 'Using the Collections' **www.library. manchester.ac.uk/search-resources/guide-to-special-collections /methodist/using-the-collections** has a page listing 'Printed Lists of Ministers and Lay People'. On the same website, some of these lists have been brought together in the 'Index of Methodist Ministers'. This gives names, denominations, dates of commencement in the ministry and dates of death.

The more important printed lists include:

- Garlick, Kenneth B. *Mr Wesley's preachers: an alphabetical arrangement of Wesleyan Methodist preachers and missionaries and the stations to which they were appointed, 1739-1818.* (Pinhorns for the World Methodist Historical Society [British Isles], 1977).
- Hall, Joseph. *Hall's circuits and ministers: an alphabetical list of the circuits in Great Britain, with the names of the ministers in each circuit from 1765 to 1885: from 1913 to 1923*, ed. T.G. Hartley. (Methodist Publishing House, 1925).
- *Ministers and probationers of the Methodist Church, formerly Wesleyan, Primitive and United Methodist: with the appointments in chronological and alphabetical order: also lists of the presidents, vice-presidents and the secretaries of the several conferences, together with an alphabetical list of deceased.* Revised to the . . . Conference of 1932–[1968]. Irregular. (Methodist Publishing House, 1933–69). Only Wesleyan Methodists are included in the earliest volume.
- Leary, William. *Ministers & circuits in the Primitive Methodist Church: a directory . . . being an alphabetically arranged directory of all Primitive Methodist ministers and the circuits they served, from 1819 to the date of death, or if still living to the date of superannuation.* (World Methodist Historical Society, 1990. Supplement, 1993).

A number of similar lists have been digitized online. Links to these are provided at:

• Methodist Heritage: Online books: Lists of Ministers and their Circuits
**www.methodistheritage.org.uk/research-online-books-ministers-and-circuits.htm**

There are a number of biographical dictionaries of Methodists. These include:

• Beckerlegge, Oliver A. *United Methodist ministers and their circuits: being an arrangement in alphabetical order of the stations of ministers of the Methodist New Connexion, Bible Christians, Arminian Methodists, Protestant Methodists, Wesleyan Methodist Association, Wesleyan Reformers, United Methodist Free Churches and the United Methodist Church, 1797-1932.* (Epworth Press, 1968)
• Hall, Joseph. *Memorials of Wesleyan Methodist ministers, or, the yearly death roll from 1770 to 1840.* (Haughton & Co., 1876). Taken from the minutes of Conference
• Michell, William John. *Brief biographical sketches of Bible Christian ministers and laymen . . . .* (Beresford Press, 1906).
• *Methodist local preachers' who's who, 1934: a complete record of the lives and careers of Methodist local preachers.* (Shaw Publishing, 1934).
• Stevenson, G.J. *Methodist worthies: characteristic sketches of Methodist preachers of the several denominations, with historical sketch of each connexion.* 6 vols. (Thomas C. Jack, 1884–6).
• *Who's who in Methodism, 1933: an encyclopaedia of the personnel and departments, ministerial and lay in the United Church of Methodism.* (Methodist Times and Leader, 1933).
• Garlick, Kenneth B. *Garlick's Methodist registry, 1983.* (Edsall, c.1983).

Pages listing 'Methodist Ministers entering the Ministry post 1932',

'Methodist Ministers of the United Methodist Church', etc., can be found at:

- My Methodist History: People
  **www.mymethodisthistory.org.uk/category/people**

Biographical notices of about 1,300 individuals, both ministers and laymen, are recorded in:

- The Methodist Archives Biographical Index
  **www.library.manchester.ac.uk/search-resources/guide-to-special-collections/methodist/using-the-collections/biographicalindex**

Obituaries for one Methodist denomination are indexed in:

- Lloyd, Gareth. *Index of Obituaries of members of the Wesleyan Methodist Association, 1838-1857 . . .* (John Rylands University Library, 1993).

For female Methodists, consult:

- Researching Women in Methodism
  **www.library.manchester.ac.uk/search-resources/guide-to-special-collections/methodist/using-the-collections/researching-women-in-methodism**

See also:

- Graham, E. Dorothy. *Chosen by God: a list of the female travelling preachers of early Primitive Methodism.* (Wesley Historical Society, 1989).

A variety of donation lists, recording the names of many Methodists, are available. The most important of these is the

Wesleyan Methodist Historic Roll (see below, pp.176–8), but there are others. See:

• Lenton, John H. 'Sources for the history of British and Irish Methodism and genealogy: some printed donation lists', *Proceedings of the Wesley Historical Society* 55(2), 2005, pp.43–52. See also 55(3), 2005, pp.121–2.

As already noted, the minutes of Conference include obituaries of all Methodist ministers, although these are primarily concerned with their work in the church and do not necessarily give any information about their families. The same applies to the many obituaries which can be found in Methodist magazines (see below, p.173). MARC also has registers of (mainly) Wesleyan Methodist candidates for the ministry, with associated papers and a collection of Methodist New Connexion preachers' certificates.

A variety of other original sources, many of them held by MARC, may yield information about individual Methodists. For the eighteenth century, the letters, diaries and papers of the Wesley brothers mention many itinerant preachers and lay people. Much of this material is in print (see above, pp.52–3). MARC also holds the personal papers of several hundred ministers and Methodist laymen. The letters of Jabez Bunting, the most prominent Methodist of the nineteenth century, have been published:

• Ward, W.R., ed. *The Early Correspondence of Jabez Bunting, 1820-1829*. Camden 4th series, 11. (Royal Historical Society, 1972).
• Ward, W.R., ed. *Early Victorian Methodism: the correspondence of Jabez Bunting, 1830-1858*. (Oxford University Press, 1976).

Much information can also be found in the archives of theological colleges and especially in their admission registers and examination results. MARC holds the archives of the Wesleyan Methodist Richmond Theological Institute, 1834–1971 and of the Primitive Methodist Hartley Victoria College, 1876–1963. Both of these trained ministers for the Methodist Church after union in 1932.

## METHODIST EDUCATION

Methodists have been active in the education of children, and founded a number of their own schools. The archives of these schools can sometimes be found in local record offices, although they may sometimes, as at Shebbear College, still be with the school. MARC holds the archives of a number of schools which were attended by the children of ministers and prominent laymen, including Kingswood School in Bristol, whose register has been published:

• Hastling, A.H.A., ed. *Register of Kingswood School*. (3rd ed. Brentford, 1923).

The National Children's Home (now known as Action for Children) was another Methodist enterprise. For information about the children it has cared for, visit:

• Action for Children: Genealogy Service
**www.actionforchildren.org.uk/what-we-do/records-and-support/genealogy-service**

Some of the children in its care were sent to Canada; for information about them, see:

• Young Immigrants to Canada
**https://personal.uwaterloo.ca/marj/genealogy/children/Organizations/stephenson.html**

Other archives relating to the National Children's Home may be found by consulting the union catalogues listed above, pp.28–9.

## METHODIST MISSION

Methodists conducted missions to all five continents in the nineteenth century. The major Methodist denominations all had their own missionary societies, the oldest of which was the Wesleyan Methodist Missionary Society, founded in 1818. After Methodist union in 1932, all of these societies joined together to form the Methodist Missionary Society. Its records, together with those of its predecessor societies, are now held by SOAS (see p.73). For details, see:

• Mundus: (Wesleyan) Methodist Missionary Society/Methodist
  Church Overseas Division Archive
  **www.mundus.ac.uk/cats/4/910.htm**

The archives include many letters from missionaries serving overseas, together with candidates' papers and a range of administrative papers. Incidentally, they also include copies of the (Wesleyan) Methodist Conference minutes, 1744–1976. The entire archive has been microfilmed and is available in a few major research libraries as:

• *Methodist Missionary Society Archives on Microfiche*. 24,281 fiche.
  IDC, 1981–3.

For the history of Methodist Missionaries, see:

• Pritchard, John. *Methodists and their Missionary Societies, 1760-
  1900.* (2 vols. Ashgate, 2013–14).

Other work from the project which resulted in this volume is available at:

• Methodist Missionary History Project
  **www.methodistheritage.org.uk/missionaryhistory-
  historyproject.htm**
  A register of British Methodist missionaries, 1769–2003, is being planned for this site.

A number of books relating to Methodist missionaries have been digitized and are linked to at:

• Methodist Heritage: Online books: Missionary Work
**www.methodistheritage.org.uk/research-online-books-missionary-work.htm**

## METHODIST PERIODICALS
Methodists have published numerous periodicals, so many that a separate pamphlet is required to list them:

• Rose, E. Alan. *A Checklist of British Methodist Periodicals*, Methodist study guide 1. (Wesley Methodist Historical Society, 1981).

Altholz (above, p.56) may also be consulted. A list of magazines officially published is included in:

• Cumbers, Frank. *The Book Room: the story of the Methodist Publishing House and Epworth Press*. (Epworth Press, 1956).

The earliest Methodist magazine was begun by Charles Wesley himself. The *Arminian Magazine* (1778–97) became the *Methodist Magazine* (1798–1821) and then the *Wesleyan Methodist Magazine* (1822–1914). Most Methodist denominations had their own magazines, for example, the *Methodist New Connexion Magazine* (1798–1907), the *Bible Christian Magazine* (1822–1907) and the *Primitive Methodist Magazine* (1821–98). There were also a number of weekly newspapers. The *Methodist Recorder* commenced in 1861 and still continues.

A number of Methodist journals have been digitized and are available online (pay-per-view).[3] These include *The Arminian/Methodist/Wesleyan Methodist Magazine*, *Primitive Methodist Magazine*, the *Watchman* and the *Minutes of Conference*. See:

• Wesleyan and Primitive Methodist periodicals
**www.britishonlinearchives.co.uk** (search 'Wesleyan' and scroll down)

Many journals carried obituaries of ministers and laymen. These were primarily concerned with the religious activities of their subjects, and do not always give much genealogical information. Two indexes to Methodist obituaries have been published:

- Jackson, F.M. *An index to the memoirs, obituary notices and recent deaths, together with the references to the local histories of Methodism, as contained in the 'Arminian Magazine', 1778-1797, the 'Methodist Magazine', 1798-1821 and the 'Wesleyan Methodist Magazine' 1822-1839.* Rev. ed. by T.E. Brigden. (Wesley Historical Society, 1909–10). Issued with the *Proceedings of the Wesley Historical Society*, Vol. 7.
- Leary, William. *An index to the memoirs, obituaries and biographies as contained in the Wesleyan Methodist magazines, 1840 to 1932.* (William Leary, 1984).

## METHODIST LIBRARIES, RECORD OFFICES, & INSTITUTIONS

There are a variety of libraries and record offices holding Methodist collections. They are listed in:

- *Directory of Methodist Libraries.* Rev. ed. (Applied Theology Press, 1999).

See also:

- Methodist Archives and Libraries: How to Find Them – and How to Use Them **www.methodistheritage.org.uk/archives-libraries-methodist.htm**

### Methodist Archives and Research Centre

The importance of MARC has already been emphasized. It is based in the John Rylands Library in Manchester. In addition to the Conference archives, it holds the correspondence and papers of thousands of prominent Methodists, including the Wesley brothers. There are also many diaries, sermons, hymnbooks and circuit plans. The extensive printed books collection includes many local histories and biographies. An up-to-date summary of archival holdings can be found at:

• Methodist Collections
  **www.library.manchester.ac.uk/search-resources/guide-to-special-collections/methodist**

See also:

• Lloyd, Gareth. *Guide to Methodist resources and research opportunities at the University of Manchester.* (John Rylands University Library, 2009).
• *Methodist Archives: catalogues, handlists, bibliographies and some important reference works.* (John Rylands University Library of Manchester, 1986).
• Riley, David Woodward. 'The Methodist Archives and Research Centre', *Bulletin of the John Rylands University Library of Manchester* 60, 1977–8, pp.269–74.

### Manchester Wesley Research Centre

The work of MARC is closely supported by this centre, which also has a library (including many theses on Methodism), publishes *Wesley and Methodist Studies* (bi-annual, 2009– ), runs seminars and conferences and provides other research facilities:

• Manchester Wesley Research Centre
  **www.mwrc.ac.uk**

### Oxford Centre for Methodism and Church History

This institution holds a number of major collections. The extensive archives of Westminster College, which opened in 1851 as a Methodist training college and merged with Oxford Brookes University in 2000, includes much information concerning its staff and students. The library of the Wesley Historical Society is discussed below. The Centre also holds the papers of a number of leading twentieth-century Methodists and has an art collection which includes many Methodist portraits and other memorabilia. For details, visit **http://history.brookes.ac.uk/Research/Centre-for-Methodism-and-Church-History/**

### Wesley College, Bristol
The College until recently held many letters and papers of Methodist worthies, including the Wesleys. These have now been deposited in MARC. Details are given in:

- Henderson, Janet. 'The special collections and manuscripts held at Wesley College, Bristol', *Wesley Historical Society Bristol Branch bulletin* 91, 2005, pp.1–8.
- McCulloch, Diarmaid. 'Manuscript collections at Wesley College, Bristol: a handlist', *Proceedings of the Wesley Historical Society* 43, 1981–2, pp.95–6. See also McCulloch's catalogue at **https://rylandscollections.files.wordpress.com/2015/01/wesley-college-bristol-archive-catalogue.pdf**

### John Wesley's Chapel, The New Room, Bristol
A collection of about 4,000 books is held. Visit: **newroombristol.org.uk/Library**

   See also:

- Spittal, C.J. 'The New Room Library', *Wesley Historical Society Bristol Branch Bulletin* 91, 2005 (irregular pagination).

### Methodist Central Hall, Westminster
The church has its own Archives Centre, which holds local circuit records, together with a collection of memorabilia. It also holds the Wesleyan Methodist Historic Roll, which records the names of over 1,000,000 people who donated a guinea to the Wesleyan Methodist Twentieth Century Fund between 1899 and 1909. This fund was used to build Central Hall. The roll serves as a census of Methodists throughout the country. Further details are given in:

- Ratcliffe, Richard. *The Wesleyan Methodist historic roll.* Basic facts about . . . series. (Federation of Family History Societies, 2007).

*John Wesley's New Room, Bristol.*

*Westminster Central Hall.* (Courtesy Wikimedia)

The amounts collected from each individual chapel, arranged by circuits and districts, is recorded in:

• *Report of the twentieth century fund*. (Wesleyan Methodist Church, c.1910).

**Wesley Historical Society**
This Society's library is the second-largest specialist collection of Methodist books in the country. It holds in excess of 10,000 items, including correspondence, circuit plans, research notes and personal papers of individual Methodists. It is administered by the Oxford Centre for Methodism and Church History (see above). Details are given on the Society's website, which also includes information concerning the society itself, its regional branches and a list of the contents of recent *Proceedings*:

• Wesley Historical Society
  **www.wesleyhistoricalsociety.org.uk**

Much Methodist historical research has been published in the Society's *Proceedings*. These have been digitized at **www.biblical studies.org.uk/articles_whs_12.php**. Printed indexes are also available:

• Vickers, John A. *Wesley Historical Society general index to the proceedings, vols. I-XXX and publications I-IV (1897-1956)*. (1960). A further volume covers Vols. 31–50 (including book reviews in Vols. 26–50).

The Society's Yorkshire Branch has an extensive library, held amongst the Special Collections of the University of Huddersfield. For its catalogue, visit **http://heritagequay.org/archives/WHS/**. Some other regional branches also have their own libraries.

**The Historical Society of the Methodist Church in Wales**
This society's journal, *Bathafarn* (bilingual in English and Welsh), has been digitized at:

- Welsh Journals Online
  **http://welshjournals.llgc.org.uk**

**The Methodist Church Archives and History Committee**
Current information on developments in Methodist archives are recorded in:

- *Methodist archives: the annual newsletter of the Archives and History Committee of the Methodist Church.* (2006– ).

**Independent Methodist Resource Centre**
The archives of the Independent Methodist Connexion are described by:

- Dolan, John A. 'The archives of the Independent Methodists', *Proceedings of the Wesley Historical Society* 49(4), 1994, pp.122–3.

**Methodist Museums**
There are also a number of Methodist Museums. An extensive library, including many works on Primitive Methodism, is held by:

- Englesea Brook Chapel and Museum
  **www.engleseabrook-museum.org.uk/history.asp**
  Click 'Library' to search the catalogue.

Other museums include:

- Epworth Old Rectory: Home of the Wesleys
  **www.epwortholdrectory.org.uk/index.php**
- Wesley's Chapel: Museum of Methodism
  **www.wesleyschapel.org.uk/education.htm**

**FURTHER READING**
Many of the books and journal articles cited in Chapter 2 include much information on Methodist sources. A number of books are solely devoted to assisting the Methodist researcher:

- Leary, William. *My Ancestors were Methodists: how can I find out more about them?* (4th ed. Society of Genealogists Enterprises, 2005).
- Ratcliffe, Richard. *Methodist Records for Family Historians.* (The Family History Partnership, 2014).
- Swift, Wesley F. *How to write a local history of Methodism.* (5th ed., revised by Thomas Shaw and E.A. Rose. Wesley Historical Society, 1994).
- Thornborow, Philip. *A Methodist in the Family? Answers to ten frequently asked family history questions.* (Methodist Heritage, 2014).

There are also a number of useful essays and journal articles:

- Baker, Frank. 'Methodist archives', *Amateur Historian* 3(4), 1957, pp.143–9.
- Gurden, Helen. 'The Methodist parish chest', *History Workshop* 3, 1977, pp.73–9.
- Leary, William. 'The Methodist archives', *Archives* 16, 1983–4, pp.16–27.
- Lloyd, Gareth. 'Methodist Printed and Archival Research Collections: a Survey of Material in UK/USA Repositories', in Yrigoyen, Charles, ed. *T&T Clark Companion to Methodism.* (Bloomsbury, 2014), pp.369–86. Useful for its coverage of British resources in the United States as well as in the UK – but it completely ignores important resources in the UK National Archives.
- Richards, P.S. 'The Methodist church and its historical records', *Journal of Regional and Local Studies* 9(2), 1989, pp.48–52.
- Welch, C.E. 'The early Methodists and their records', *Journal of the Society of Archivists* 4, 1970–3, pp.200–11.

MARC has prepared a number of useful webpages for the guidance of researchers:

- Researching your Family History
  **www.library.manchester.ac.uk/search-resources/guide-to-special-collections/methodist/using-the-collections**
  Click title.

For a detailed, but not very accurate, listing of British Methodist sources, see:

• Calkin, Homer L. *Catalog of Methodist archival and manuscript collections. Part 6, Great Britain and Ireland*. (World Methodist Historical Society, 1985–91).

There are numerous publications on Methodist history. Only a handful can be mentioned here. For a comprehensive listing of older works, see:

• Rowe, Kenneth E. *Methodist union catalog, pre-1976 imprints*. (20 vols. in progress. Scarecrow Press, 1975– ).

A 'Bibliography of Methodist historical literature' was formerly published regularly in the *Proceedings of the Wesley Historical Society*. This has been published as an annual supplement to the *Proceedings* since 1987. The annual listings have been digitized for 1974–2007 and are linked to at **https://clivedfield.wordpress.com/publications-british-methodist-bibliography-2/**

For unpublished theses, see:

• Methodist Heritage: Theses and dissertations
**www.methodistheritage.org.uk/thesesanddissertations.htm**

Numerous books and journals related to Methodism have been digitized. Some are listed at:

• Methodist Heritage: Online Books
**www.methodistheritage.org.uk/research-online-books.htm**

Numerous reference works are available. The most recent, which identifies many earlier works, is:

• Yrigoyen, Charles, ed. *T&T Clark Companion to Methodism*. (Bloomsbury, 2014). Includes a useful survey of archival sources and a bibliography.

See also:

- Abraham, William J., & Kirby, James E., eds. *The Oxford Handbook of Methodist Studies*. (Oxford University Press, 2009).

A number of useful essays placing British Methodism in its international context are included in:

- Gibson, William, Forsaith, Peter, & Wellings, Martin. *The Ashgate Companion to World Methodism*. (Ashgate, 2013).

For basic information on denominations, brief biographies, outline local histories and a variety of other topics, consult:

- Vickers, John A., ed. *A Dictionary of Methodism in Britain and Ireland*. (Epworth Press, 2000). An internet version of this book is available at: **dmbi.wesleyhistoricalsociety.org.uk**

Another brief dictionary, with a useful bibliography, is provided by:

- Yrigoyen, Charles, Jr., & Warrick, Susan. *Historical Dictionary of Methodism*. (Scarecrow Press, 1996).

A number of bibliographies list books dealing with particular denominations:

- Beckerlegge, Oliver A. *A bibliography of the Bible Christians*. United Methodist Bibliographic Series 2. (Gage, 1988).
- Beckerlegge, Oliver A. *A bibliography of the Methodist New Connexion*. United Methodist Bibliographic Series 1. (Gage, 1988).
- Hatcher, Stephen. *A Primitive Methodist bibliography*. (The author, 1980).
- Beckerlegge, Oliver A. *A bibliography of the United Methodist free churches*. United Methodist Bibliographic Series 4. (Gage, 1988).

- Beckerlegge, Oliver A. *A bibliography of the United Methodist Church*. United Methodist Bibliographic Series 5. (Gage, 1988).
- Beckerlegge, Oliver A. *A bibliography of the Wesleyan Methodist Association and other branches*. United Methodist Bibliographic Series 3. (Gage, 1988).

Anyone interested in Methodist heritage should consult the wide range of pages at:

- Methodist Heritage
  **www.methodistheritage.org.uk**

Many useful pages for genealogists, including 'My Primitive Methodist ancestors', 'My Wesleyan Methodist ancestors' and 'My Bible Christian Ancestors' can be found at:

- My Methodist History
  **www.mymethodisthistory.org.uk**

The best introduction to Methodist history worldwide is:

- Hempton, David. *Methodism: empire of the Spirit.* (Yale University Press, 2005).

Useful histories of UK interest include:

- Davies, Rupert, & Rupp, Gordon, eds. *A history of the Methodist church in Great Britain.* (4 vols. Epworth Press, 1965–88). There is an extensive bibliography in Vol. 4.
- Hempton, David. *The religion of the people: Methodism and popular religion, c.1750-1900.* (Routledge, 1996).
- Kent, Joan. *Wesley and the Wesleyan religion in eighteenth-century Britain.* (Oxford University Press, 2002).

There are a number of works dealing with particular denominations. Some of the better ones include:

- Beckerlegge, Oliver A. *The United Methodist Free Churches: a study in freedom*. (Epworth Press, 1957).
- Bowmer, John C. *Pastor and People: a Study of Church and Ministry in Wesleyan Methodism from the Death of John Wesley (1791) to the death of Jabez Bunting (1855)*. (Epworth Press, 1975).
- Dolan, John. *The Independent Methodists: a History*. (James Clarke, 2005).
- Jones, William H. *History of the Wesleyan Reform Union* (Epworth Press, 1952). Digitized at **www.thewru.com/about-us/history/one-is-your-master.php**.
- Lander, John K. *Itinerant Temples: Tent Methodism 1814-1832*. (Paternoster Press, 2003).
- Lysons, Kenneth. *A Little Primitive: Primitive Methodism from macro and micro Perspectives*. (Church in the Market Place Publications, 2001).
- Shaw, Thomas. *The Bible Christians, 1815-1907*. (Epworth Press, 1965).
- Werner, Julia Stewart. *The Primitive Methodist Connexion: its background and early history*. (University of Wisconsin Press, 1984).
- Wickes, Michael J.L. *The West Country Preachers: a new history of the Bible Christian Church (1815-1907)* (Appledore, 1987).

There are many local studies of Methodism. One which may serve as a model is:

- Ambler, R.W. *Ranters, revivalists and reformers: Primitive Methodism reformers: Primitive Methodism and rural society: South Lincolnshire 1817-1875*. (Hull University Press, 1989).

## Chapter 6

# EVANGELICAL CHURCHES OF THE EIGHTEENTH AND NINETEENTH CENTURIES

Evangelical activity in the eighteenth and nineteenth centuries was greatly influenced by the Wesleyans, but they did not have the field all to themselves. George Whitefield and Benjamin Ingham had also been members of the Holy Club in Oxford. Doctrinal differences prevented them from working closely with the Wesleys. The latter believed that Christ died for all, following the view of the Dutch theologian Arminius. Whitefield and Ingham both held to the older Calvinist position – which was also held by most of the old Dissent – that Christ died only for the elect. Whitefield and Ingham both founded their own denominations, as did the Countess of Huntingdon. In Wales, the Calvinistic Methodist Church (now the Presbyterian Church of Wales) traces its origins even further back, to the preaching of Griffith Jones of Llanddowror, Carmarthenshire, who began his ministry as early as 1708.

The Moravians also played an important role in the evangelical revival. John Wesley first experienced the Holy Spirit in a Moravian meeting. However, Wesley and the Moravians went their separate ways – although Benjamin Ingham united some of his societies with the Moravians.

Almost a century after John Wesley's death, General Booth founded the Salvation Army. This was another offshoot of Methodism. Booth had been a minister of the Methodist New Connexion, but found that he was unable to answer his call to evangelism within the structures of his denomination. The Salvation

Army was begun as a missionary society, rather than as a separate denomination.

A number of other missionary organizations began in much the same way as the Salvation Army, but did not develop into separate denominations. Some were organized by the mainstream denominations; mention has already been made of Methodist and Congregational Home Missions. Others were ecumenical in character. For example, the London City Mission, was established in 1835 to work amongst London's poor and destitute. Many obituaries of its pre-1910 missionaries, together with an index to the *LCM Magazine* 1836–1968, are included on its website, which also provides information concerning its extensive archival collection. Visit:

- London City Mission: Archives
  **www.lcm.org.uk/our-mission/archives**

## A. CALVINISTIC METHODISTS

George Whitefield had as much energy as John Wesley and travelled extensively. He founded many churches, but lacked Wesley's organizational abilities and failed to create a structure which could have held his English Calvinistic Methodist churches together. Most became Congregationalist and their records are similar to those of other Congregational churches (see Chapter 3).

In Wales, the Calvinistic Methodists survive as a separate denomination, now known as the Presbyterian Church of Wales. It was served by the journal *Y Drysorfa* (1831–1968). Connexional records are held in the National Library of Wales and are described in:

- Davies, K. M. 'The archives of the Calvinistic Methodist or Presbyterian Church of Wales', *National Library of Wales Journal*, 5(1), 1947, pp.13–49.

See also the description at:

- Archives Wales
  **www.archivesnetworkwales.info**
  Search 'Calvinistic Methodist Archives'.

Much information from the archives, and other historical research, is published in:

- *Cylchgrawn Cymdeithas Hanes y Methodistiaid Calfinaidd: the Journal of the Calvinistic Methodist Historical Society*. (1916– ).

Records of particular churches are held by both the National Library of Wales and by local record offices.

For the history of Calvinistic Methodism in the eighteenth century, see:

- Jones, David Ceri, Schlenther, Boyd Stanley, & White, Eryn Mant. *The Elect Methodists: Calvinistic Methodism in England and Wales, 1735-1811*. (University of Wales Press, 2012).

Whitefield worked closely with Selina, the Countess of Huntingdon, who had considerable influence on Dissent and built up her own connexion. However, she failed to make adequate provision for its future. Some of her churches became Congregationalist; others joined the Free Church of England. A remnant of the Connexion still survives **www.cofhconnexion.org. uk**. For its early history and details of relevant archives, see:

- Harding, Alan. *The Countess of Huntingdon's Connexion: a sect in action in eighteenth-century England*. (Oxford University Press, 2003).

The records of two early London churches are printed in:

- Welch, Edwin, ed. *Two Calvinistic Methodist chapels 1743-1811: the London Tabernacle and Spa Fields chapel*. (London Record Society 11, 1975).

See also:

- Welch, Alan, ed. *Sion Chapel, Ashbourne, letters and papers 1801-1817*. (Derbyshire Record Society 25, 1998).

*Selina Hastings, Countess of Huntingdon (1707–91), founder of the Huntingdon Connexion.*

The Countess founded a college for training ministers at Trevecca (sometimes spelt Trevecka, or Trefeca). This subsequently moved, becoming Cheshunt College, which is now amalgamated with Westminster College, Cambridge **www.westminster.cam.ac.uk/ rcl/research-archives**. College archives hold many files on individual students. The College also holds the Countess's

Connexional archives and many of her personal letters. They are calendared in:

• Welch, Edwin. *Calendar and index of Cheshunt College archives.* (List & Index Society special series 14, 1981).

See also:

• Welch, Edwin, ed. *Cheshunt College: the early years: a selection of records.* (Hertfordshire Record Publications 6, 1990).

For Trevecca College, see:

• Nuttall, Geoffrey F. *The Significance of Trevecca College, 1768-91.* (Epworth Press, 1969). Reprinted in Nuttall's *Studies in English Dissent.* (Quinta Press, 2002), pp.285–303.

For letters concerning Trevecca, see:

• Schlenther, Boyd Stanley, & White, Eryn Mant, ed. *Calendar of the Trevecka letters.* (National Library of Wales, 2003).

Students' names are listed in:

• Nuttall, Geoffrey F. 'The students of Trevecca College 1768–91', *Transactions of the Honourable Society of Cymmrodorion* 1967, part II, pp.249–77.

## B. INGHAMITES

Benjamin Ingham was another member of the Oxford 'Holy Club' who founded a denomination. The Inghamites were active in four northern counties: Yorkshire, Westmorland, Lancashire and Nottinghamshire. Now only a handful of chapels survive. MARC holds conference minutes for 1750–60 (MA3128). A handful of registers were deposited with the Registrar General and are now in The National Archives RG4 (see above, pp.67–8). A detailed guide to the few remaining chapel records, including transcripts of a number of registers and lists of names mentioned in conference minutes is provided by:

• Oates, P.J. *My Ancestors were Inghamites*. (Society of Genealogists Enterprises, 2003).

See also:

• List of Inghamite Chapels
  **https://en.wikipedia.org/wiki/List_of_Inghamite_chapels**

### C. MORAVIANS

The Moravians traced their origin to fifteenth-century Bohemia. After the Protestant defeat at the Battle of the White Mountain in 1620, they became a persecuted minority, eventually finding refuge in Saxony in 1722 under the protection of Count Zinzendorf. The Count believed that all men could be saved by faith in the atoning work of Christ and argued that such faith was shared by many denominations. The Moravian emphasis was placed on love and behaviour, rather than on doctrine, and they were happy to work with other denominations. Moravians regarded themselves as a religious society, rather than a separate denomination – a position shared by the Wesleyans.

Most Moravians were members of 'Societies', which had their own ministers and buildings, but which went to the parish church for communion. A smaller number were members of separate 'congregations'. There were also four 'settlements' – at Fulneck (Yorkshire), Fairfield (Lancashire), Ockbrook (Derbyshire) and Bedford. Members of settlements lived together as a disciplined community, following their own vocations.

Moravian congregations kept a variety of records. Registers of births, marriages and deaths, were maintained to a high standard Congregation books list members (and their children) by date of admission and generally include birth dates, whether married, and occupations. They may also indicate former religious affiliations. Congregation calendars, compiled annually, also list members, but few survive. Congregation diaries record services held, information on the movement of members and visitors, relations with other denominations, and other information that was felt to be worth recording. The information in them overlapped with the minutes of the Conference of Elders, which record the names of all applicants for membership, the appointment of office bearers, reports from daughter societies and other matters. These records may have been deposited in local record offices, or in the Moravian Archives. A search of the union catalogues listed on pp.28–9 may be worthwhile. Nineteen pre-1837 registers of births, marriages and deaths are deposited in The National Archives (see above, pp.67–8). A collection of documents from the Bedford Moravian church is printed in:

- Welch, Edwin, ed. *The Bedford Moravian church in the eighteenth century: a selection of documents.* (Bedfordshire Historical Record Society 68, 1989).

The Moravian Church British Province Archives hold many printed books relating to the worldwide history of the Church. There are a number of biographies, hymn books, theological works and periodicals. The latter include *The Messenger* (1873–90), succeeded by the *Moravian Messenger* (1890– ).

The Archives also hold the central records of the British Province. These include minutes of Synod and its committees, the archives of the Society for the Furtherance of the Gospel, records relating to Moravian property and much correspondence. Summaries of congregational diaries were sent to headquarters on the continent. There are transcripts of materials from the Continental headquarters of the church. The archives of many defunct congregations are also held. These include the archives of the chapel at Fetter Lane, which played a particularly significant role in Moravian history. For more details, see:

- Archives of the Moravian Church British Province
  **www.moravian.org.uk/index.php/church-house/church-archives**

- Blewett, Paul, & Reynolds, Simon. 'The Moravian Church Archives and Library', *Journal of the Society of Archivists* 22(2), 2001, pp.193–203.

Many transcripts of material taken from the Archives are held by the John Rylands Library. See:

- Moravian Church Manuscripts
  **www.library.manchester.ac.uk/search-resources/guide-to-special-collections/atoz/moravian-church-manuscripts**

**Further Reading**
- Mason, J.C.S. *The Moravian Church and the missionary awakening in England, 1760-1800.* (Boydell Press, 2001).
- Podmore, Colin. *The Moravian church in England, 1728-1760.* (Oxford University Press, 1988).
- Stead, Geoffrey, & Stead, Margaret. *The Exotic Plant: a history of the Moravian Church in Great Britain, 1742-2000.* (Epworth Press, 2003).

### D. THE SALVATION ARMY
William Booth was an ordained Methodist minister, who resigned his pastorate because he found Conference rules restricted his ability to follow his calling as an evangelist. In 1865, he took charge of the East London Mission. It subsequently became the Christian Mission. In 1879 it changed its name again, becoming the Salvation Army. As an army, it adopted military terminology, terming its ministers officers and its local organizations Corps.

Booth intended to establish an evangelistic organization, rather than a separate denomination. The Army involved itself in a wide range of social issues, promoting medical work, organizing orphanages, adoption and fostering, sponsoring emigration and tracing missing persons. It also established Corps throughout the world. Corps are listed in the annual *Salvation Army Yearbook* (1906– ). The standard history of the Army is:

*Salvation Army Band in Brisbane, Australia, 1950.* (Courtesy Wikimedia)

• Randall, Robert, et al. *The History of the Salvation Army.* (5 vols. Thomas Nelson & Son, 1947–68). v.1. 1865–1878. v.2. 1878–1886. v.3. 1883–1953: social reform and welfare work. v.4. 1886–1904. v.5. 1904–1914.

See also:

• Walker, Pamela J. *Pulling the Devil's Kingdom Down: the Salvation Army in Victorian Britain.* (University of California Press, 2000).

Since 1907, each Corps has maintained a 'Corps history book', in which is recorded all its activities. Corps also maintain registers of dedications (births), marriages, and promotions to glory (deaths). Marriage registers are duplicates of the civil registers (see above, p.66). Soldiers' rolls record the names of members, as do the records of various Corps organizations, such as bands. Most Corps records are still kept by Corps officers; few have been deposited in local record offices.

The officers of the Salvation Army are its clergy. Records for most officers appointed since 1878 are held centrally, although recent records are closed under the Data Protection Acts and some early records have been lost. The Army provides a guide to 'Officers Records' on its website (below). Officers trained at William Booth College, which maintained registers of students, giving details such as full name, date of birth, the corps at which the cadet (officer in training) was a soldier before entering training, previous occupation, languages spoken, other skills and details of first appointment as an officer. Career records trace officers' careers in the Army, although many have been lost prior to 1941. *Dispositions of Forces* are annually published directories of current corps and Territorial Headquarters posts in the UK and Ireland, identifying officers in post. These and a variety of other sources, are held by:

• Salvation Army International Heritage Centre
  **www.salvationarmy.org.uk/international-heritage-centre**

A brief guide to Army records for family historians is provided by:

• Wiggins, Ray. *My Ancestors were in the Salvation Army: how can I find out more about them?* (3rd ed. Society of Genealogists Enterprises, 2007).

For the records of Salvation Army girls' homes, see:

• Clark, David. 'The Salvation Army girls' statement books', *Genealogists' Magazine* 27(3), 2001, pp.129–32.

In the first half of the twentieth century, the Salvation Army was heavily involved in promoting emigration. A 'subject guide' to its emigration records is downloadable from:

• The New Exodus: The Salvation Army and Emigration
  **www.salvationarmy.org.uk/history/blog12**

*Chapter 7*

# FOREIGN CALVINIST CHURCHES

Many foreign churches have established themselves in England and especially in London. We have already considered the Moravians, who arrived in the eighteenth century. In earlier centuries, most foreign churches were Calvinistic, although by 1700 Greek Orthodox and Lutherans were also present. Not all of these churches were Nonconformist. Some accepted the oversight of bishops; some used a French translation of the English prayer book. Others preferred to keep their Presbyterian structures and to be Nonconformist. All received valuable backing from the government, especially during the reigns of Elizabeth I and William III – although Archbishop Laud under Charles I was less enthusiastic. In return, the Huguenots in particular played a major role in the country's economic and military success.

The earliest foreign church was established in 1550, when Edward VI granted the church of the Austin Friars to Dutch, Flemish and Walloon 'strangers'. The Walloons were subsequently granted a chapel in Threadneedle Street. Some members of these churches were refugees, but many were probably economic migrants. Many fled when Mary ascended the throne and closed their churches down in 1553. On the accession of Elizabeth, they were re-opened under the supervision of the Bishop of London.

The Duke of Alva's appointment as Captain General in the Low Countries in 1567 signalled the beginning of severe persecution on the continent. Many Dutch and Walloon Protestants fled to England. Some French Huguenots followed after the Massacre of St

*The St. Bartholomew's Day Massacre, 1572, painted by François Dubois.*

Bartholomew in 1572, but the majority of refugees went to Geneva rather than England. By the end of Elizabeth's reign there were many foreign Protestant churches in London and ten in the provinces.

In the early seventeenth century, these churches gradually declined as refugees assimilated to the host country. From the beginning, some refugees had joined the Church of England rather than the churches of their own communities. The children and grandchildren of refugees had less reason than their forebears to attend a French or Dutch speaking church, and Archbishop Laud wanted to close them down in the 1630s. However, the Revocation of the Edict of Nantes in 1685 caused over 40,000 French Huguenots to seek refuge in England. These refugees revitalised the churches which received them. They also founded new churches. In Devon, for example, churches were established at Plymouth, Stonehouse, Exeter and Barnstaple.

It is not always easy to establish the existence of a Huguenot church in a particular place. They may have left no records and it may be necessary for the local historian to use Church of England diocesan and other sources to identify them. A detailed listing of known churches is included in Chater's guide mentioned below (p.203). See also:

- Gwynn, Robin. 'The distribution of Huguenot refugees in England', *Proceedings of the Huguenot Society of London* 21(5), 1970, pp.414–36; 22(6), 1976, pp.509–68.

There is much information in the State Papers Domestic (see above, pp.43–4) regarding Huguenots. Various lists of aliens and registers of denizations, have been published. Many of those mentioned in them were refugee Huguenots. See:

- Cooper, W.D., ed. *Lists of foreign protestants and aliens resident in England, 1618-88*. (Camden Society old series 82, 1862).
- Kirk, R.E.G., & Kirk, Ernest F., eds. *Returns of aliens dwelling in the City and suburbs of London from the reign of Herny VIII to that of James I*. (4 pts. Publications of the Huguenot Society of London 10, 1900–8).
- Page, W., ed. *Letters of denization and acts of naturalization for aliens in England, 1509-1603*. (Huguenot Society Publications 8, 1893).
- Scouloudi, Irene, ed. *Returns of strangers in the Metropolis, 1593, 1627, 1635, 1639: a study of an active minority*. (Huguenot Society of London Quarto series 57, 1985).
- Shaw, W.A., ed. *Letters of denization and acts of naturalization for aliens in England and Ireland 1603-1700*. (Huguenot Society Publications 18, 1911. This is continued for the period 1701–1800 in vol.27, 1923 and supplemented by vol.35, 1932).

Governmental encouragement of the Huguenots may be illustrated from the records of the Royal Bounty, which have been listed by Smith (see below, p.202). Between 1686 and 1804, grants were made from the Privy Purse to poor distressed Huguenots. These grants were administered by various committees and commissioners and were channelled through the Huguenot churches. Most surviving records are registers of recipients, which include many personal details. The Huguenot Society library has a partial name index. For those relieved through the Threadneedle Street church, reference may be made to:

- Hands, A.P., ed. *French protestant refugees relieved through the Threadneedle Street church, London, 1681-1687*. (Huguenot Society of London Quarto series 49, 1971).

For a detailed discussion of the archive held by the Huguenot Society, consult:

- Le May, Keith. 'London records of poor relief for French Protestants, 1750-1850', *Proceedings of the Huguenot Society of London* 26(1), 1994, pp.71–82.

Some records were held in Guildhall Library (but have since been transferred to London Metropolitan Archives). See:

- Thomas, A.H. 'The documents relating to the relief of French Protestant refugees, 1693 to 1718, preserved in the Records Office at the Guildhall, London', *Proceedings of the Huguenot Society of London* 12(4), 1922, pp.263–87.

The Nonconformist Huguenot churches generally followed the classic Presbyterian manner of church government. They were run by elected elders, deacons and ministers, sitting in Consistory. Consistories dealt with a wide range of matters – worship, ministerial arrangements, relief of the poor and of refugees, finance, seating, membership, marriage, discipline, etc. Many of their minutes survive, and some have been published. A full list is given in:

- Spicer, Andrew. 'The Consistory records of reformed congregations and the exile churches', *Proceedings of the Huguenot Society* 28(5), 2007, pp.640–63.

For an example of published minutes, consult:

• Gwynn, Robin, ed. *Minutes of the Consistory of the French Church of London, Threadneedle Street, 1679-1692.* (Huguenot Society of Great Britain and Ireland Quarto series 58, 1994).

A variety of other records were kept, not dissimilar to those of other Nonconformists. Registers of baptisms, marriages (sometimes including banns) and burials were usual. However, Huguenot marriage registers ceased in 1753 (see above, p.62). And few Huguenot churches had burial grounds, so most burials are recorded in parish registers.

Huguenot registers were generally deposited with the Registrar General in 1841 and are now in The National Archives, class RG 4. These have been digitized and can now be viewed on the BMD Registers website (see above, pp.67–8). They have also all been published, mostly by the Huguenot Society (see below).

In addition to vital events, Huguenot registers sometimes also include records of *reconnaissances* and *tesmoignages*. *Reconnaissances* were public confessions of failure to uphold Calvinistic principles under persecution. *Tesmoignages* are certificates of good standing granted to church members when they moved to a different church. These records may also be found occasionally in separate books. Some have been published:

• Minet, William, & Minet, Susan, eds. *Livre des tesmoignages de L'Eglise de Threadneedle Street, 1669-1789.* (Publications of the Huguenot Society of London 21, 1909).
• Minet, William, & Minet, Susan, eds. *Livre des conversions et des reconnaissances faites a l'eglise Francoise De la Savoye, 1684-1702.* (Publications of the Huguenot Society of London 22, 1914).

A variety of membership lists may also be available. Elders had to keep lists of the members in their districts. Membership lists might show the contributions each member made. Pew lists recorded seating arrangements.

Consistories worked closely with each other. In London, the Dutch, French and Italian churches regularly met together in a joint assembly, the Coetus. Its minutes (together with those of the Italian Consistory) are published in:

• Boersma, O., & Jelsma, A.J., eds. *Unity in multiformity: the minutes of the Coetus of London, 1575 and the Consistory minutes of the Italian church of London, 1570-1591*. (Publications of the Huguenot Society of London 59, 1997).

All of the foreign churches submitted to their Colloques, whose acts have been published in:

• Chamier, Adrian Charles, ed. *Les Actes des Colloques de Eglises Françaises et des Synodes des Eglises Etrangères refugièes en Angleterre, 1581-1654*. (Publications of the Huguenot Society of London 2, 1890).

Ministers are listed in:

• Manchee, W.H. 'Huguenot clergy list, 1548-1916', *Proceedings of the Huguenot Society of London* 11, 1915–17, pp.263–92. See also pp.387–99.

In addition to the Royal Bounty, discussed above, Huguenots dispensed much charity. Schools and apprentices were funded, and the earliest Friendly Societies were Huguenot institutions. The best known charitable institution is probably La Providence – the Huguenot French Hospital. For a brief history, see:

• Marmoy, Charles F.A. 'La Providence: the French Hospital during two and a half centuries', *Proceedings of the Huguenot Society of London* 21(4), 1969, pp.335–54.

Its inmates are listed in:

• Marmoy, Charles F.A., ed. *The French Protestant Hospital: extracts from the archives of La Providence relating to inmates and applications for admission, 1718-1957 and to recipients of and applications for the Coqueau charity, 1745-1901.* (2 vols. Huguenot Society of London publications Quarto Series 52-3, 1977).

Another volume is devoted to:

• Marmoy, Charles F.A., ed. *The case book of La maison de charitie de Spittlefields, 1730-41.* (Huguenot Society of London publications Quarto Series 55, 1981).

A much higher proportion of Huguenot records are in print than is the case with the records of other denominations, thanks to the work of the Huguenot Society, which has so far printed sixty-nine volumes in its two Quarto series of publications. The Society also publishes the *Huguenot Society Journal* (2013– ), which continues its *Proceedings* (1885–2012) and includes many articles of relevance to both family and local historians. *Huguenot Families* (1999–2008) catered for family historians, but ceased publication. The titles of all the Society's publications can be viewed by clicking 'Huguenot Society Publications' at:

• Royal Historical Society: National History and Record Societies **http://royalhistsoc.org/publications/national-history-and-record-societies**

Digitised images of the *Proceedings* are available for members only on the Society's webpage. The *Proceedings* and the Quarto series are indexed in:

• *New General Index to the Proceedings and Quarto Series, 1885-2007.* (Huguenot Society, 2011).

There is also a detailed surname index to the *Proceedings* in:

• Gandon, John. *Master index to the Proceedings of the Huguenot Society of Great Britain and Ireland, volume I-XXV, 1886-1997.* (Huguenot Society, 1998). Quarto Series.

The Society's library is now administered with the special collections of University College London. For details, visit:

• UCL Library Services: Huguenot Library
  **www.ucl.ac.uk/library/special-collections/huguenot**

The library has a substantial book collection and holds many works which are difficult to find elsewhere. It also holds the archives of many churches, together with records of the Royal Bounty, the French Hospital and other Huguenot institutions. There are numerous collections of family papers, together with Family Research files and Wagner Pedigrees for some Huguenot families. The Society's website (below) has a page on the Huguenot Library. See also:

• Bradford, Kenneth. 'The Huguenot Library: hidden treasure revealed', *Proceedings of the Huguenot Society* 26(3), 1995, pp.343–9.
• Scouloudi, Irene. 'Some Huguenot records in London collections', *Archives* 11(51), 1974, pp.152–6.

Detailed catalogues are provided by:

• Gray, Irvine R. *Huguenot manuscripts: a descriptive catalogue of the remaining manuscripts in the Huguenot Library*. (Huguenot Society of London Quarto series 56, 1983).
• Harcourt Williams, M. *Huguenot archives: a further catalogue of the remaining manuscripts in the Huguenot Library*. (Huguenot Society of London Quarto series 61, 2008).
• Smith, Raymond. *Records of the Royal Bounty and connected funds: the Burn donation and the Savoy church in the Huguenot Library, University College London*. (Huguenot Society of London Quarto series 51, 1974).

Further information about the Society is provided by its own web-page, which has a useful guidance page for family historians:

• Huguenot Society of Great Britain and Ireland
**www.huguenotsociety.org.uk**

## FURTHER READING

A detailed guide to sources, including notes on all known Huguenot settlements, is provided by:

• Chater, Kathy. *Tracing your Huguenot Ancestors: a guide for family historians*. (Pen & Sword, 2012).

See also:

• Currer-Briggs, Noel, & Gambier, Royston. *Huguenot Ancestry*. (Phillimore, 1985).

There are a number of general histories and collections of articles relating to the Huguenots:

• Cottret, B. *The Huguenots in England: immigration and settlement. c.1550-1700*. (Cambridge University Press, 1991).
• Gwynn, Robin D. *Huguenot Heritage: the history and contribution of the Huguenots in Britain*. (Routledge & Kegan Paul, 1985).
• Vigne, Randolph, & Gibbs, Graham C., eds. *The stranger's progress: integration and disintegration of the Huguenot and Walloon refugee community, 1567-1889*. (Issued as *Proceedings of the Huguenot Society of Great Britain and Ireland* 26(2), 1995).
• Vigne, Randolph, & Littleton, Charles, eds. *From strangers to citizens: the integration of immigrant communities in Britain, Ireland and colonial America, 1550-1750*. (Huguenot Society of Great Britain & Ireland/Sussex Academic Press, 1991).

For an example of a good local study, see:

• Spicer, Andrew, ed. *The French-speaking reformed community and their church in Southampton, 1567-c.1620*. (Huguenot Society New series 3, 1997. Also published as Southampton Record series 39).

# *Chapter 8*

# OTHER DENOMINATIONS AND SECTS

There are numerous denominations and sects that have not yet been mentioned. Most were founded in the nineteenth and twentieth centuries, although a few go back further than that. This survey is based on published and internet sources that are readily available. Consequently, some denominations get little mention. The more exclusivist sects take no interest in their history and, indeed, keep their archives secret. They prefer, on theological grounds, to look to the future. Others do not have a central structure and consequently the preservation of local church archives is a matter for voluntary church officers. Archives may not be cared for or accessible and it can be very hit or miss whether they survive.

Local record offices have sometimes been successful in obtaining deposits, especially of registers and it is worth checking the union catalogues listed on pp.28–9. It is always worth checking whether any original documents are held in church safes, or by church officers. Even if nothing survives, some evidence is likely to be available in the documents discussed in Chapter 2. Details of archival resources for some groups, for example, the Church of Christ Scientist, and the Jehovah's Witnesses, do not seem to be publically available.

## A. CATHOLIC APOSTOLIC CHURCH
This denomination (sometimes referred to as Irvingites after one of its founders) was founded in 1835 by a group of aristocrats and ministers (both Anglican and Nonconformist), who had been meeting informally for some years to discuss prophecies of the

millennium. The Second Coming was believed to be imminent, the Holy Spirit was thought to be speaking through contemporary prophets, and the Lord was thought to have called a new apostolate to bring the church back to His ways. Services were characterized by an elaborate liturgy, combined with speaking in tongues and prophecy – although charismatic activities were brought under increasingly strict control. Government was very hierarchical, firmly under the control of the Twelve Apostles, who were the only people with the power to ordain ministers. Apostles were not replaced when they died. Consequently, no more priests could be ordained and the denomination slowly died out.

Tierney (below) includes lists of churches in the UK at various dates. Records are not easy to trace, as the church regarded them as secret. The papers of Henry Drummond, who was one of the Apostles, have been deposited in the Bodleian Library and are described by Lively (below).

Records from Bradford have been deposited with the West Yorkshire Archives Service and form the basis of Tierney's article. They include a 'General Register' of communicants, of Angels, Priests, Deacons, Deaconesses and the departed in the faith; of those refusing pastoral care; and persons unfaithful. This register also includes a 'record of events 1867–1931'. There are also registers of Services, 1880–5 and 1948–59. A number of other collections are listed by Discovery and other union catalogues (see pp.28–9).

**Further Reading**
The authoritative study of the denomination's history, including a detailed review of previous historical accounts, is:

- Flegg, Columba Graham. *Gathered under Apostles: a study of the Catholic Apostolic Church.* (Oxford University Press, 1992).

See also:

- Newman-Norton, Seraphim. *The Time of Silence.* (4th ed. Lulu, 2005).
- Shaw, P.E. *The Catholic Apostolic Church, sometimes called Irvingite: a historical study.* (New York, 1946).

Useful journal articles include:

- De Gruchy, Jane. 'The Catholic Apostolic Church in Bradford, 1872-1882', *Local Historian* 36(1), 2006, pp.29–41.
- Lively, R. L. 'Bodleian sources for the study of two nineteenth-century millenarian movements in Britain', *Bodleian Library Record* 13, 1991, pp.491–500. Also discusses sources for the Latter Day Saints.
- Tierney, David. 'The Catholic Apostolic Church: a study in Tory millenarianism', *Historical Research* 63(152), 1990, pp.289–315.

## B. CHRISTADELPHIANS

The Christadelphians – the Brothers of Christ – were founded by John Thomas, an English migrant to America, in the mid-nineteenth century. They are an exclusivist sect, who do not accept the Trinity or practise infant baptism; nor will they serve in the police or the army. The Ecclesia is the local congregation; there is minimal central organization and no paid pastorate. For a brief summary of their beliefs and practices, visit:

- Wikipedia: Christadelphians
  **https://en.wikipedia.org/wiki/Christadelphians**

The sociology of the sect is discussed in:

- Wilson, Bryan Ronald. *Sects and Society: a sociological study of three religious groups in Britain.* (William Heinemann, 1961). This also deals with Christian Scientists and the Elim Four Square Gospel Church (a Pentecostal denomination).

Very few archives relating to the sect have been deposited, although the University of Huddersfield has recently acquired what it describes as the 'Christadelphians Library' (**http://heritagequay. org/archives** – search 'Christadelphians'). Most archives identified in The National Archives Discovery catalogue relate to Christadelphian interaction with government, e.g. in planning matters. Papers relating to conscientious objection during both world wars may mention them.

## C. CHRISTIAN BRETHREN
The Brethren movement began in Dublin in 1828, although they are sometimes known as the Plymouth Brethren. They are conservative evangelicals. The denomination split in 1848 into 'open' and 'exclusive' groupings over disciplinary issues. They now have Assemblies in most English counties. Their movement was originally inspired by J.N. Darby, whose works are available online:

• John Nelson Darby
  **http://bibletruthpublishers.com/john-nelson-darby-jnd-collections/lucl13**

Brethren have a low visibility, but their numbers are substantial. There were thought to be over 1,200 'open' Brethren churches in England in 1913 and many more 'exclusivists'. In 1959, it was estimated that there were between 75,000 and 100,000 'open' Brethren.[1]

The Brethren are characterized by the lack of an ordained ministry and a high degree of participation by members in worship and organization. There is no central organization. It may be useful to consult the movement's periodicals. *Word and Work* (1875–98) was published weekly. Monthlies included *The Witness* (1870–1980) and *The Harvester* (1923– ). The *Missionary Reporter* was the movement's missionary journal, commencing in 1853.

James Hudson Taylor, who established the China Inland Mission (now known as OMF International) in 1865, was closely associated with the Brethren. The archives of his Mission are now held by SOAS, together with the personal papers of its founder and of some of his fellow workers. They are described at **www.mundus.ac.uk**.

George Müller established the Müller Orphan Homes in Bristol. The records of 17,000 orphans are available; for details, visit:

• Müllers Orphan Records
  **www.mullers.org/orphanrecords**

*Boxer Rising Memorial of the China Inland Mission.*

*The China Inland Mission even produced its own banknotes.*

Thomas Barnardo was another member of the Brethren who worked with children. The charity he founded now describes itself as the 'UK's leading children's charity'. Its webpage outlines its history and offers a 'genealogy service' for tracing former Barnardo children:

• Barnardo's: Our History
  **www.barnardos.org.uk/what_we_do/our_history.htm**

Assemblies may be identified in trade directories (see p.57), which may use terms such as 'mission hall' or 'gospel hall' to identify Brethren chapels. Trust deeds (see pp.47–8) may provide useful information. Local newspapers may report on Brethren activities. Assembly archives may include marriage registers. Infant baptism is not practised, so there are no baptismal registers. A few Assemblies have deposited archives in local record offices. The most important collection for the denomination, held by the John Rylands Library, is described by:

• Christian Brethren Collection
  **www.library.manchester.ac.uk/search-resources/guide-to-special-collections/christian-brethren-collections**

The collection includes records for several Assemblies, together with a substantial number of Brethren periodicals and the papers of many individual Brethren. Its website also links to a variety of other resources.

The Brethren Archivists and Historians Network publishes the *Brethren Historical Review* (formerly *BAHN Review*). Many articles from the *Review* are available on its website, which also has a bibliography. page and some useful links. See:

• Brethren Archivists and Historians Network
  **www.brethrenhistory.org/?pageid=723**

**Further Reading**
For a detailed guide to studies of the Brethren, see:

• The Brethren: a bibliography of secondary studies
  **www.library.manchester.ac.uk/search-resources/guide-to-special-collections/christian-brethren-collections/printed-material/bibliography**

The best introduction to Brethren history is:

• Grass, Tim. *Gathering to His Name: the Story of the Open Brethren in Britain and Ireland.* (Paternoster, 2006).

See also:

• Coad, F.R. *A History of the Brethren movement: its origin, its worldwide development and its significance for the present day.* (2nd. ed. Paternoster Press, 1976).

For nineteenth-century origins, consult:

• Rowdon, H.H. *Origins of the Brethren Movement 1825-1850.* (Pickering & Inglis, 1967).

One hundred Brethren biographies are included in:

• Pickering, Hy. *Chief Men Among the Brethren.* (2nd ed. Pickering & Inglis, 1931).

For information on sources, consult:

• Brady, David 'The Christian Brethren Archive in the John Rylands University Library of Manchester', in Giorgi, Lorenza & Rubboli, Massimo, eds., *Piero Guicciardini, 1808-1886: un riformatore religioso nell' Europa dell' ottocento.* (Firenze, 1988), pp.175–91.

- Wilson, John. 'Sources for the history of the Christian Brethren', *Local Historian* 14(8), 1981, pp.478–80.

## D. CHURCHES OF CHRIST

Sometimes known as the Campbellites, the Churches of Christ came together in the early nineteenth century under the influence of Alexander Campbell and others. Their aim was to restore New Testament Christianity, and their theology is sometimes termed Restorationist. Their *Millennial Harbinger and Voluntary Church Advocate* began publication in 1835. Congregations were independent and practised adult baptism. They were run by elders and deacons. Support was concentrated in the Midlands and Lancashire. In the nineteenth century, there were no paid ministers, although some congregations did have full-time evangelists. Many Churches of Christ joined the United Reformed Church in 1980. Those that did not unite formed:

- The Fellowship of Churches of Christ
  **https://fellowshipofchurchesofchrist.wordpress.com**.

The central records of the denomination, 1842–1981, were formerly in the Cadbury Research Library at the University of Birmingham, but are now held by Westminster College, Cambridge. They are currently being catalogued. Two websites offer brief histories of the denomination:

- World Convention: National Profiles: United Kingdom
  **www.worldconvention.org/resources/profiles/united-kingdom/**
- The Fellowship of Churches of Christ: Our Story
  **https://fellowshipofchurchesofchrist.wordpress.com/our-story/**

For a more detailed account, see:

- Thompson, D.M. *Let Sects and Parties Fall: a short history of the Association of Churches of Christ in Great Britain and Ireland.* (Berean Press, 1980).

Useful journal articles include:

- Ackers, Peter. 'The "Protestant ethic" and the English Labour movement: the case of the Churches of Christ', *Labour History Review* 58(3), 1993, pp.67–72.
- Billington, L. 'The Churches of Christ in Britain: a study in nineteenth-century sectarianism', *Journal of Religious History* 8(1), 1974, pp.21–48.
- Thompson, D.M. 'Churches of Christ in the British Isles, 1842-1972: a historical sketch', *Journal of the United Reformed Church History Society* 1(1), 1973, pp.23–34.

### E. CHURCH OF JESUS CHRIST OF LATTER DAY SAINTS (MORMONS)

The Latter Day Saints (LDS), more commonly known as Mormons, are an American sect who base their theology on the Book of Mormon, supposedly written by the angel Moroni and revealed to Joseph Smith. They began to evangelize the United Kingdom in 1837 and encouraged their converts to emigrate to Utah. In 1850, there were over 30,000 British members. Mormons encourage converts to baptize their dead ancestors, and consequently keep many records. These are centralized in Utah, but many are available on microfilm through the LDS worldwide network of Family History Centres.

The LDS local congregation is termed a 'branch'. Several branches form a Stake, which regularly meets in Conference. Conference records include minutes of meetings, accounts, membership tallies and other items.

Each branch keeps records of its members, including their places and dates of birth, baptism (into the Mormon church), removal (whether in England or to Utah), and excommunication. The earliest membership records had no standard format or content. Local LDS officers used blank journals to record members' names, parentages, dates of birth and LDS baptisms, details of marriages, children, emigration and a variety of other matters. From 1877, standard printed forms began to be used; these were drastically revised in 1900, 1922 and 1941. Many include a membership number, which remained with the member for life, and may be useful for tracing information in other sources.

Detailed financial records record contributions made by individual members to various church funds. Between 1907 and 1983, annual genealogical reports were compiled by the church's units recording information for those who had experienced certain events during the year, not just baptism, marriage and burial, but also blessing, ordination and a number of other experiences.

A variety of other sources are detailed in Ian Waller's book (see below). Many of these sources, including the membership records described above, are combined in the 'early church information file', which is available on microfilm. This is an alphabetical index containing c.1,500,000 entries, drawn from a wide range of sources and ranging in date from the 1830s to the early twentieth century.

Most of these sources are only available through the LDS Family History Library and its Family History Centres. See:

• Introduction to LDS Family History Centers
  **https://familysearch.org/learn/wiki/en/Introduction_to _LDS_Family_History_Centers**

Some Mormon sources are also available at **www.ancestry.co.uk**, but these are primarily of American interest. The University of Oxford's Bodleian Library hold microfilms of manuscript histories and historical reports of the British Mission, 1837–1969, the originals of which are held by the Church Archive Centre in Utah. Reports of conferences and missionary activities, instructions to missionaries and emigrants, etc., are printed in the *Latter-Day Saints' Millennial Star* (1840– ), also in the Bodleian Library.

**Further Reading**
For a detailed guide to Mormon sources, see:

• Waller, Ian. *My Ancestor was a Mormon*. (Society of Genealogists Enterprises, 2011).

For material deposited in the Bodleian Library, see:

- Lively, R. L. 'Bodleian sources for the study of two nineteenth-century millenarian movements in Britain', *Bodleian Library Record* 13, 1991, pp.491–500.

There are a number of useful histories:

- Bloxham, V. Ben, et al, eds. *Truth will prevail: the rise of the Church of Jesus Christ of Latter-Day Saints in the British isles, 1837-1987.* (Church of Jesus Christ of Latter Day Saints, 1987).
- Jensen, Richard L., & Thorp, Malcolm R., eds. *Mormons in early Victorian Britain.* Publications in Mormon studies 4. (University of Utah Press, 1989). Includes Whittaker, David J. 'Mormonism in Victorian Britain: a bibliographic essay'.
- Taylor, P.A.M. *Expectations Westward: the Mormons and the emigration of their British converts in the nineteenth century.* (Oliver & Boyd, 1965).

For some useful journal articles, see:

- Benson, Evva C., & Doxey, Cynthia. 'The ecclesiastical census of 1851 and the Church of Jesus Christ of Latter-day Saints', *Local Historian* 34(2), 2004, pp.66–79.
- Cannon, M.H. 'Migration of English Mormons to America', *American Historical Review* 52(3), 1947, pp.436–55.

Local studies include:

- Bartholomew, Ronald E. 'Babylon and Zion: Buckinghamshire and the Mormons in the Nineteenth Century', *Records of Buckinghamshire* 48, 2008, pp.231–54.
- Cartwright, Catherine. 'Latter-Day Saints in South Derbyshire 1842-1857', *Derbyshire Archaeological Journal* 128, 2008, pp.123–35.
- Fleming, Stephen J. 'The religious history of the British Northwest and the Rise of Mormonism', *Church History* 77(1), 2008, pp.37–104.

## F. CHURCH OF THE NAZARENE

This is a twentieth-century movement with its roots in the Wesleyan tradition and the Holiness Movement. There are currently about ninety congregations, mainly in the north. Its history is recounted in:

• Noble, A. *Called to be Saints: a centenary history of the Church of the Nazarene of the British Isles, 1906-2006*. (Didsbury Press, 2006).

For the denomination's UK archives, see:

• Archives at NTC [Nazarene Theological College] **https://nazarene.ac.uk/about-us/ntc-archives/**

## G. FAMILY OF LOVE

The Family of Love (sometimes known as Familists) were one of the handful of separatists groups that existed prior to the Civil War. They were followers of Hendrik Niclaes, a sixteenth-century Dutch merchant and mystic. Most of its followers were from East Anglia, although some of Elizabeth's Yeomen of the Guard were Familists. They were a secretive sect, but many Familists have been identified by:

• Marsh, Christopher. *The Family of Love in English Society, 1550-1630*. (Cambridge University Press, 1994).

## H. FREE CHURCH OF ENGLAND

The Free Church of England was founded in 1844 in order to counter the Oxford Movement, and to enable evangelicals to continue their work in an Anglican setting. It had over forty congregations in 1960. Some churches have deposited their records in local record offices.

The denomination's history is recounted in:

• Fenwick, John R.K. *The Free Church of England: introduction to an Anglican tradition*. (T. & T. Clark International, 2004).

## I. GLASITES

The first meeting house of this group was established in Dundee in 1733. Its founder, Reverend John Glas, had been a Presbyterian minister. Glas was a Calvinist and aimed to form a community of saints exercising strict discipline in self-governing congregations. His son-in-law, Robert Sandeman, founded churches in England and in America; his followers were known as Sandemanians. Central beliefs of the Glasites include the view that Christ's Kingdom is purely spiritual and wholly separate from the state.

The denomination died out in the twentieth century. Records of some churches, together with lists of members, correspondence and sermons, are held by the University of Dundee's Archives Service; for details, visit **www.archiveshub.ac.uk** (search 'Glasite).

## J. JEHOVAH'S WITNESSES

This movement grew out of Adventist traditions in the USA. Members were originally known as Bible Students, but in 1931 the present name was adopted. They proclaim the imminence of the Millennium, deny the Trinity, and have an extremely hierarchical structure, although there is no paid ministry. Congregations meet in Kingdom Halls. About twenty congregations make up a circuit and ten circuits make up a district. Each has an overseer. The national headquarters in each country is called the Bethel. There is no publicly available central archive, but some Kingdom Halls have deposited late twentieth-century registers in local record offices.

### Further Reading

- Beckford, James A. *The Trumpet of Prophecy: a sociological study of Jehovah's Witnesses*. (Blackwell, 1975).
- Penton, M. James. *Apocalypse Delayed: the story of Jehovah's Witnesses*. (2nd ed. University of Toronto Press, 1997).

## K. MUGGLETONIANS

This tiny sect takes its name from Lodowicke Muggleton, who, during the Interregnum, proclaimed himself one of the two last prophets foretold in the Book of Revelation. The last Muggletonian

*Lodowicke Muggleton (1609–98), founder of the Muggletonians, painted by William Wood.*

trustee, Philip Noakes, bequeathed the sect's archives to the British Library in 1979. Muggletonian history is recounted in:
- Hill, Christopher, Reay, Barry, & Lamont, William. *The World of the Muggletonians.* (Temple Smith, 1983).
- Lamont, William. *Last Witnesses: the Muggletonian history, 1652-1979.* (Aldershot: Ashgate, 2006).

See also:

- Wikipedia: Muggletonianism
  https://en.wikipedia.org/wiki/Muggletonianism

Many Muggletonian texts are digitized at:

• Muggletonian.org.uk
  **http://muggletonian.org.uk**

### L. PENTECOSTALISTS

Pentecostalism is a twentieth-century phenomenon, although its roots go back to Wesleyanism and the Holiness Movement. It is characterized by baptism in the Spirit and speaking in tongues. Worship is informal, designed to be open to the movement of the Holy Spirit. Pentecostalism began in America in 1901. Revival began in Wales in 1904. In 1907, an English Methodist who had experienced the revival at first hand in America brought it to Sunderland. Early converts were encouraged to remain in their own denominations. The revival was not about questioning the specific doctrines of particular denominations; rather it was about rejecting dry formalism in religion. Nevertheless, denominational structures gradually emerged. The Apostolic Faith Church was founded in 1908. Elim Four Square Gospel Alliance was founded in 1915 in Ireland and had 350 churches by 1979. In 1924, the British Assemblies of God came together and now have over 600 churches. There are a variety of other Pentecostal denominations, for example, the Apostolic Church and the Vineyard.

Local churches have not looked after their archives very well and researchers may find that they have to rely on newspapers and oral testimony. A few congregations have deposited their archives – and especially registers – in local record offices. The major institution for the study of Pentecostalists is the Donald Gee Centre. It holds the archives of The Assemblies of God (1925–present) and the Elim Pentecostal Church (1915–95). It also holds many early periodicals, the minutes of the Pentecostal Missionary Union, various collections of letters and sermons and the archives of the Fountain Trust (which promoted charismatic renewal between 1964 and 1980). Its website has a link to some digitized material. See:

• The Donald Gee Archive: The British Pentecostal and
  Charismatic Archive
  **http://donaldgeearchive.com**

See also:

• Mattersey Hall: Pentecostal Archives
  **www.matterseyhall.com/resources/donaldgeearchives**

There is also some material at:

• Regents Theological College Learning Resource Centre
  **www.regents-tc.ac.uk/Groups/244561/Library.aspx**

Many historic Pentecostalist documents can be read at:

• The Revival Library
  **www.revival-library.org**

**Further Reading**
Many useful books and journal articles are listed by:

• Bibliographies For Pentecostal and Charismatic Studies
  **http://artsweb.bham.ac.uk/aanderson/Pentecost/
  bibliographies.htm**

The standard dictionary of Pentecostalism worldwide (with an American bias) is:

• Burgess, Stanley M., ed. *The New International Dictionary of Pentecostal and Charismatic Movements.* (Rev. ed. Zondervan, 2002).

For the history of Pentecostalism in Britain, see:

• Anderson, Allan H., & Hollenweger, Walter J., eds. *Pentecostals after a Century: global perspectives on a movement in transition.* (Sheffield Academic, c.1999).
• Hollenweger, Walter J. *The Pentecostals.* (SCM Press, 1969).
• Kay, William K. *Pentecostals in Britain.* (Paternoster Press, 2000).

- Kay, William K. *Apostolic Networks of Britain: new ways of being church*. (Paternoster Press, 2007).
- Randall, Ian M. *Evangelical Experiences: a study in the spirituality of English evangelicalism 1918-1939*. (Paternoster Press, 1999).

For a local study, see:

- Homan, R. 'Age of miracles: the Pentecostal revival in Sussex', in Kitch, M.J., ed. *Studies in Sussex Church History*. (Leopards Head Press, 1981), pp.223–42.

## M. SANDEMANIANS
See Glasites

## N. SEVENTH DAY ADVENTISTS
This denomination was founded in the USA in the mid-nineteenth century, after the 'Great Disappointment' of 1844, when the predicted Second Coming did not happen. Its name is based on its practice of worshipping on the seventh day, i.e. Saturday. The church's British Union Conference is currently developing the 'BUC Historical Archive' **www.adventisthistory.org.uk**. The website includes a number of digitised historical documents, including the denomination's principal journal, the *Messenger*, for 1923–50, and a number of local church histories.

A few Adventist churches have deposited their archives in local record offices (see pp.28–9 for union catalogues). World Wide Advent Missions have deposited some records with the London Metropolitan Archives.

For the Adventists' own view of their denomination's history in the British Isles, see:

- A Century of Adventism in the British Isles
  **www.adventisthistory.org.uk/documents/Centuryof Adventism.pdf**

## O. SWEDENBORGIANS (OR, THE NEW CHURCH)
Emanuel Swedenborg was a Swedish mystic whose writings

combined elements of theosophy and pantheism. A group of his disciples came together to form the New Church at Great Eastcheap in 1789. The denomination's first conference was held in 1791. By 1851, the Swedenborgians were established in thirty-seven districts, with a particular strength in the West Riding. For the early history of the denomination, see:

- Hindmarsh, Robert. *Rise and Progress of the New Jerusalem Church in England, America and other part*, ed. Edward Madeley. (Hodson & Son, 1861).
- Lineham, Peter J. 'The Origin of the New Jerusalem Church in the 1780s', *Bulletin of the John Rylands University Library of Manchester* 70(3), 1988, pp.109–21.

An up-to-date history of the Swedenborg Society is provided by:

- Lines, Richard. *A History of the Swedenborg Society, 1810-2010.* (South Vale Press, 2010).

See also:

- New Church History
  **www.newchurchhistory.org**
- Wikipedia: The New Church
  **https://en.wikipedia.org/wiki/The_New_Church**

For the origins of the denomination, see:

- Lineham, Peter J. 'The Origins of the New Jerusalem Church in the 1780s', *Bulletin of the John Rylands University Library of Manchester* 70(3), 1988, pp.109–21.

An 'introduction to the Archives' can be found at:

- Swedenborg Society: The Library
  **www.swedenborg.org.uk/library**

# NOTES

## Chapter 1: The History of Nonconformity

1. John, 17, v.22.

2. See, for example, Evans, Nesta. 'The descent of Dissenters in the Chiltern Hundreds', in Spufford, Margaret, ed. *The World of Rural Dissenters, 1520-1725.* (Cambridge University Press, 1995), pp.288–308; Bernard, G.W. *The Late Medieval English Church: vitality and vulnerability before the break with Rome.* (Yale University Press, 2013), pp.206–35.

3. For the argument that they were merely a figment of their opponents' fearful imagination, see Davies, J.C. *Fear, Myth and History: the Ranters and the Historians.* (Cambridge University Press, 1987).

4. Angell, Stephen W., & Dandelion, Pink. *The Oxford Handbook of Quaker Studies.* (Oxford University Press, 2013), p.26.

5. Doel, William. *Twenty Golden Candlesticks, or, a history of Baptist Nonconformity in Western Wiltshire.* (B. Lansdown & Son, 1890. Reprinted Wiltshire County Council/Wiltshire Family History Society, 2005).

6. Brockett, Allan. *Nonconformity in Exeter, 1650-1875.* (University of Manchester Press, 1962), p.22.

7. Hill, Christopher. *A Turbulent, Seditious and Factious People: John Bunyan and his Church 1628-1688.* (Clarendon Press, 1988), pp.293–4.

8. For the names of rebels, see Wingfield, W.M. *The Monmouth Rebels, 1685.* (Somerset Record Society, 79, 1985). See also the same author's *The Monmouth Rebellion: a social history.* (Moonraker Press, 1980).

9. Pope, Robert, ed. *T & T Clark Companion to Nonconformity.* (Bloomsbury, 2013), p.65.

10. On sacrament certificates, see Raymond, Stuart A. *Tracing your Church of England Ancestors.* (Pen & Sword, forthcoming).

11. Bebbington, David W. *Victorian Nonconformity*. (Cambridge: Lutterworth Press, 2011), p.20.

12. Ibid., p.17.

13. Heard, R.M. *Methodism in Kilkhampton*. (The author, 1985).

## Chapter 2: Sources for Nonconformity

1. See Raymond, Stuart A. *Parish Registers: a History and Guide*. (Family History Partnership, 2009).

2. See Raymond, Stuart A. *The Census 1801-1911: a Guide for the Internet Era*. (Family History Partnership, 2009).

3. See Raymond, Stuart A. *The Wills of our Ancestors: a Guide to Probate Records for Family & Local Historians*. (Pen & Sword, 2014).

4. More detailed information on the internet from a Nonconformist perspective is provided by Mills, S.J. *Probing the Past: a Toolbox for Baptist Historical Research*. (Baptist Historical Society, 2009).

5. For its records, see Dixhoorn, Chad Van, ed. *The Minutes and Papers of the Westminster Assembly, 1643-1652*. (5 vols. Oxford University Press, 2012).

6. For the academies of the old Dissenters, see below, p.81.

7. A number of surveys undertaken by Nonconformists in the late seventeenth and eighteenth centuries are discussed below, pp.78–9.

8. For Thompson's survey of 1773, see below, p.79.

9. Appleby, David J. 'From ejectment to Toleration in England, 1662-89', in Sell, Alan P.F., ed. *The Great Ejectment of 1662: its antecedents, aftermath and ecumenical significance*. (Pickwick Publications, 2012), p.111.

10. These are available online at **http://parlipapers.chadwyck. co.uk/marketing/index.jsp** (if you are a member of an institution which has a subscription).

11. Bunyan, John. *Grace abounding & the life and death of Mr. Badman*. (Everyman's Library, 1928), pp.103–29.

12. Turner, J. Horsfall, ed. *The Nonconformist Register of Baptisms, Marriages and Deaths compiled by the Revs. Oliver Heywood & T.Dickenson, 1644-1702, 1702-1752, generally known as the Northowram or Coley register, but comprehending numerous notices of Puritans and anti-Puritans in Yorkshire, Lancashire, Cheshire, London, &c., with lists of popish recusants, Quakers, etc.* (J.S. Jowett, 1881).

13. Bebbington, David. *Victorian Nonconformity*. (Cambridge: Lutterworth Press, 2011), p.27.

### Chapter 3: The Three Denominations
1. For links to digitized images of this magazine, visit **http://online books.library.upenn.edu**
2. Marsh, Christopher. *The Family of Love in English Society, 1550-1630*. (Cambridge University Press, 1994).

### Chapter 4: The Quakers
1. Pope, Robert, ed. *T & T Clark Companion to Nonconformity*. (Bloomsbury, 2013), p.68.
2. Stevens, Sylvia. 'Travelling Ministry', in Angell, Stephen W., & Dandelion, Pink. *The Oxford Handbook of Quaker Studies*. Oxford Handbooks in religion and theology. (Oxford University Press, 2013), pp.292–305.
3. Monthly Meetings for Church Affairs were not necessarily co-extensive with Monthly Meetings for Worship, although they often were.
4. For Quarter Sessions records of proceedings against Quakers, see above, pp.48–9.
5. Registers from the Meetings at Tivetshall, Norfolk and Oakham, Rutland, arrived late and can be found in The National Archives, RG 8/81 & RG 8/87-9.

### Chapter 5: The Methodists
1. For details, see Simon, John S. 'Elections to the Legal Hundred', *Proceedings of the Wesley Historical Society* 13(1), 1921, pp.14–21.
2. Pews in early Methodist chapels, like those in Anglican parish churches, were sometimes regarded as private property that could be sold; cf. Bretherton, F.F. 'The Sale of a Pew', *Proceedings of the Wesley Historical Society* 20(1), 1935, pp.20–3.
3. Some are also available on free sites such as those listed above, pp.27–8.

### Chapter 8: Other Denominations
1. Coad, F.R. *A history of the Brethren movement*. (Rev. ed. 1976), pp.186 & 209.

# Personal Name Index

# Place Name Index

227

# Subject Index